Acknowledgements

The author wishes to express his thanks to Stephen Nicolay for having typed the various drafts as well as the final version of this text and for his work in promoting the book.

He also wishes to thank Roger Gibbs for having studied and criticised the drafts and Nazanin McPherson for her work in research.

About the Author

John Wakelin is the author of 'The Good Life in the Good Society: an Ideology for the 21st Century' (2009) and of 'Education: Purpose and Control' (2013), both published by Arima Publishing.

WELFARE
WITHOUT
BENEFITS

John Wakelin

Published 2016 by arima publishing

www.arimapublishing.co.uk

ISBN 978 1 84549 677 7

Printed and bound in the United Kingdom

Typeset in Garamond

arima publishing
ASK House, Northgate Avenue
Bury St Edmunds, Suffolk IP32 6BB
t: (+44) 01284 700321

www.arimapublishing.com

WELFARE WITHOUT BENEFITS

Part I of this book sets out how the British social security system works and identifies many examples of waste and injustice.

Part II identifies the principles which should determine how such enterprises are managed and proposes a much fairer and more effective system.

CONTENTS

9. Concern that benefits misused

10. The Beveridge Bequest

11. Benefits for immigrants

12. Responsibility shared with local government

C. The coalition government's attempt to solve the problem – 2010-2015

D. Finding a better way

1. Basic Income – A partial solution

2. Charles Murray's proposal

3. Policy Exchange proposal for compulsory unemployment insurance scheme

4. A principled approach

Part II - A Principled Approach to Welfare - 1 Principles

A. The socialist model

1. The case for state control

2. The weaknesses of state control

3. The provision of public services

4. The target culture

5. Out sourcing

6. Is socialism dead?

B. The capitalist model

1. The case for capitalist control

2. The weaknesses of capitalism

3a) The banking crisis 2007-09 and the subsequent economic breakdown

3b) The continued misbehaviour of bankers

C. Finding a new model.

1. Prime purpose must be to serve others

2. Income must come from those served

Part II - A Principled Approach to Welfare - 2 Proposals

Part I

Britain's crazy benefits system

A. How the British social security system has operated to ensure that everyone has sufficient income.

The foundation of the welfare state was a great achievement but the passage of time, the redefinition of our values and the merely pragmatic tinkering with the system to meet current needs has created a system the weaknesses of which are clearly apparent.

The first objective of the welfare state remains the same: that the state must ensure that at all points in their lives people have sufficient income to obtain their basic physical requirements. This section contains an outline and criticism of the various ways in which the system operates.

1. The State Pension

The point at which an individual is most likely to need financial help is in old age, traditionally after a person or that person's spouse has retired from work.

The simplest way in which the state might help would be to provide a basic pension of a specific sum at a certain age – the normally accepted retirement age – for everyone. This sum would be paid for out of general taxation – as those who advocate a Citizen's Pension today suggest – and would be raised each year to take into account increased cost of living.

There are two good arguments against this. First it would either be insufficient or, if sufficient, at too high a cost to the state and thus to the taxpayer. Secondly, for people to feel a sense of independence and self respect they should, as far as possible, be responsible for their own lives; it is much better if people save a specific sum each week or month, for their employer, if there is one, to add to this and for the state to contribute too so that the sum can be invested to provide a fixed sum each week in old age.

The aim – to pay for pensions by national insurance contributions

After the Second World War, the government decided (or at least pretended) to introduce such a system of national insurance on similar lines to the partial system adopted from 1911. All employees would contribute so much from their pay with a supplement from their employer while the self-employed would contribute rather more. Men would receive a pension at 65 and women at 60.

Contributions were made weekly or monthly by all employed workers between the ages of 16 and 60 or 65 once their pay reached a specific level. The payment was a percentage of income, above the specified level and up to the Upper Earnings Limit and a lower percentage of earnings above that. The person's employer made a contribution at the appropriate percentage rate at the same time, once the worker's pay was above the specified level.

The amount of money to be paid in National Insurance contributions has of course altered frequently in the years since they were introduced. The main reason for this has been the falling value of money caused by inflation but there has also been an increase in the real value of contributions made and payments received.

In 2014 – 15 employees were expected to pay 12% of earnings above £153 pw (£663.01 pcm) until their pay reached the Upper Earnings Limit of £776.01 pw (£3,337 pcm) after which they paid 2%. The employer has been expected to pay 13.8% of the employee's earnings above £153.01 pw. Self-employed people made a larger contribution but on a similar basis. After paying National Insurance contributions for the prescribed number of years (44 for men, 39 for women until 2010) a person was entitled to a full basic pension.

In some cases a person could be credited with having made contributions even when this was not the case. If for instance someone was earning more than the Lower Earning Limit (LEL) (£111 pw in 2014-15) but not as much as the Secondary Threshold (£153.06 in 2014-15) this person was not expected to make any contributions but the earnings were noted so that entitlement to benefits was retained. If however this person earned less than the LEL there was no such credit.

The amount of pension received in 2014-15 was £113.00 but the amount for 2015-16 was set out by the DWP as follows:

Basic state pension – maximum rate £115.95

Basic State Pension based on husband's, wife's, or civil
partner's National Insurance contributions – maximum rate £69.50

Increase for an adult dependant – maximum rate £65.70

Increase for a child dependant

   - eldest child £8.00

   - each other child £11.35

Increased payment for an adult dependant was only paid if you were awarded it before 6th April 2010.

Increased payment for a child dependant was only paid if you were awarded it before 6th April 2003.

We must believe that all these minor variations in payments arise from a desire to be as fair as possible to particular groups. But if we did not know that our civil servants were people of the highest integrity we would suspect that all these variations were there to justify the employment of even more people in the DWP.

Weaknesses and injustices in the operation of the system

(a) Pretend Insurance

The basic weakness in this system is that it pretends to be a system of insurance but really is not. Contributions are paid into government funds in the same way as taxes and the government pays out the pensions. There has been some relation between payments and eventual benefit but by no means a precise one, such as would be expected in a proper insurance system. The government can decide to raise the pension above the inflation index figure if it so wishes. Indeed it became earnings related for a time from the 1960s until the 1980s and is becoming so again. In the end it's the government that decides how much you get, not the payments you have made. Thus voluntary NI contributions that people were encouraged to make to cover non-working years can, as mentioned above, simply be disregarded. This is the sort of injustice which government can safely cause since there is no outside body to force it to apply the principles of justice.

Those who paid fewer contributions for less than the prescribed period have received less pension and if they have contributed for less than 25% of this period they have not been entitled to a pension at all. The government has encouraged people in this position to make voluntary national insurance (NI) contributions to make sure that they are entitled to a full state pension when they retire. Each year HM Revenue & Customs sends out 3 million letters warning people that they face a state pension shortfall unless they top up their contributions.

More than a quarter of a million people - mostly women on career breaks, the self-employed and those working temporarily overseas – have been making voluntary payments. A later Pensions Act has however ruled that people would get the full state pension even if they had made only 30 years of contributions. The change means that many people who have stretched themselves to make full contributions have ended up out of pocket, a serious injustice which the state has ignored.

For example, someone who worked overseas for three years and kept making British national insurance contributions would end up more than £7,000 worse off than someone less prudent who didn't make any payments. The government does not intend to make any refunds.

Upon reaching the age of 80, however, everyone, including non-contributors, is entitled to a minimum 60% of the full pension. The sums paid have been raised annually in line with inflation. The main point remains. The system is unjust. It does not relate entitlement to payments in.

There were some rules but the government, if it wished, could change them however unfair the consequences might be for some. State pension provision was supposed to depend on how many years you make NIC's. To receive a full state pension men needed 44 qualifying years while women needed 39. But from April 6th 2010, a woman needed 30 NIC years to qualify, so one who turned 60 on April 5th 2010 needed 39 qualifying years and one who turned 60 a day later would need only 30. So a woman who had worked and paid in NIC for 39 years received, from April 5th 2010, no more than one who had worked and paid in for 30 years.

(b) Payment depends on where you live.

Whether or not the pension is annually updated in line with inflation depends, incredibly, on where you live. If you live in an EU country you get the increase but if you go to Australia, for instance, it may be frozen. Mr Geoff Pendlebury, in a letter to the Times (07/10/04) on behalf of such people wrote that such pensions were "frozen at the rate applicable at the time of going to live abroad in spite of having made all the necessary contributions" and comments "just because a pensioner chooses to spend his or her remaining years nearer to family who may have emigrated, he or she is penalised".

Nothing was done either by the Labour government or by the coalition that followed: in 2010 they allowed this manifest injustice to remain. In November 2013, Sheila Telford, Chairman of the International Consortium of British Pensioners, wrote to the Times: "Many pensioners wish to retire overseas, yet the Government is still dictating where British pensioners can retire to through an archaic and unjust policy. Currently, the Government freezes the pensions of British state pensioners living in a number of countries, including Australia, New Zealand, Canada and South Africa, at the rate it is when first received. More than half a million pensioners overseas are affected by frozen pensions, simply by choosing the "wrong" country to call their new home. This cruel, unjust policy means that many seniors, particularly widows and widowers, are destined to live apart from their own relatives for cost reasons".

The government took no action and on 20th October 2014 the Times published a letter from John Markham, Director of the International Consortium of British Pensioners (ICBP) in Ottawa. Mr Markham pointed out that 550,000 pensioners living overseas faced an increasing burden, having to live on a state pension frozen at the rate which applied when they left the UK. He condemned "the government's archaic, cruel and illogical policy and as Director of the ICBP, urged Mr Cameron to give these people the income they deserve".

British governments of all complexions have failed to remove this injustice.

The hard truth is that government can easily create or allow injustice in social security because it can get away with it. If we want a system that is just, it must not be run by the state.

(c) Not enough – so additional means tested payments

The amount of pension was widely recognised as insufficient for those who had no other income – and some have not even qualified for a full pension.

Governments sought to solve this problem not by an increase in the basic pension but by income support for pensioners whose total income was less than a specified figure, i.e. by means testing. So one man saves during his life to ensure that he has an investment income of at least £10 pw to supplement his basic pension. A second pensioner of similar means spends all his income on holidays, eating and drinking so that he has no savings. The second pensioner is given £10 pw by the state. The first pensioner gets nothing. He will notice that by being responsible he is no better off than his neighbour who chose not to save. Means-testing discourages responsibility and thus undermines personal character, in particular-self reliance. Government has been happy to accept this injustice.

MIG – Minimum income Guarantee

Gordon Brown, Chancellor of the Exchequer 1997 – 2007 exacerbated this injustice by introducing the Minimum Income Guarantee (MIG) in April 1999. This guaranteed all pensioners a minimum weekly income. Thus those who had saved to produce a total income at or above the level of the MIG would get no state help while those who had not bothered to do so would – hardly an encouragement to people to save and take responsibility for their own lives. Indeed the Secretary of State for Social Security at the time, Alastair Darling, accepted that a pensioner with £20 of occupational pension on top of the state pension could be just a pound or two better off than someone who saved nothing. "That's unfair, unjust and it's going to stop" he said. But why was such an unfair measure implemented? The state, sadly, often fails to concern itself with justice

Pension Credit

The Chancellor therefore decided to introduce the Pension Credit to take effect in 2003. Those pensioners with other income (such as a private pension) which, when combined with state benefits, would still be worth less than a specified sum per week would also receive a cash credit to reward them for saving in addition to the basic state pension. Those who had a weekly income of more than the minimum income guarantee but less than this specified sum would not need the original income top-up but could get the cash credit in addition to their pension. This pension credit was to be paid along with the basic state pension. By 2008/09 the pension credit ensured that each individual would be entitled to a total income of at least £124.05 pw.

In 2009 the benefit arising from pension credit was increased for those who had saved a good amount. Until then, just the first £7,600 of savings had been discounted, but from November 2009 this was increased to £10,000. As a result, some 500,000 pensioners could be up to £8 pw better off. Under the new system, for each £500 of capital over £10,000 that a pensioner had, benefit would be reduced by £1.

There were therefore two forms of pension credit, known as Guarantee Credit and Savings Credit.

By 2015, Guarantee Credit was awarded to bring up the pensioner weekly income to £151.20 for a single person and £230.85 for someone with a partner.

Savings Credit, for those who had saved money for their retirement, would in April 2015 bring in an extra £14.82 for a single person over 65 and an extra £17.43 for someone with a partner.

The age at which you can apply for pension credit was due to be 65 by 2018 and 66 by 2020. However, the savings credit part would not be available for those reaching pension age on or after April 2016.

One effect of the MIG and pension credit was that those who thought they qualified had to complete a long form or undertake a telephone questionnaire to reveal their income so that their means and entitlement could be assessed by the agents of government. Many older people found this demeaning while others were not even aware of the opportunity.

A National Audit Office report in November 2002 had found widespread ignorance about the system. Most pensioners regarded the state retirement pension as an entitlement but many still saw other payments to which they were entitled as charity and refused to apply for them. Others feared that they would be judged incapable of managing on their own.

Some mistakenly believed that the authorities would know what benefits they were entitled to and inform them. Between a quarter and a third of entitled pensioners did not claim income guarantees in the first year.

Harmful effects of means testing

The harmful effect of the means-tested Pension Credit was pointed out by Richard Harvey, chief executive of Aviva, Britain's largest insurance group, in his address as chairman of the Association of British Industries (ABI) in November 2004. It was, he said, "neither sustainable nor sensible".

"It's clear that means testing gets in the way of people saving, or saving adequate amounts for retirement" Mr Harvey said. "People simply don't know whether they're pouring their hard earned cash down the drain by saving in a private pension, because by the time they get to retirement they'd be no better off, or little better off, than someone who hadn't saved and got means tested benefits. That cannot be right".

Yet by January 2005 more than half the elderly people in the UK were entitled to means tested benefits (although many did not claim).

Statistics released by the Department of Work and Pensions (DWP) on 08.02.05 on the take up of benefits showed that as few as 63% of those eligible for a minimum income guarantee applied for the money. More than half of those who did not apply for the benefit were aged over 75 and two thirds lived in low income households. The total amount of the minimum income guarantee that was unclaimed was £1.5 billion in 2002-03, after up to 960,000 people did not claim the benefit, the DWP said.

If a pensioner, either through choice or ignorance, had not initially asked for the means tested Pension Credit but subsequently did so, then logic suggests that there should be a payment back dated to the time at which the pensioner qualified. After the 6th October 2008 however, the government refused to make back dated payments covering more than three months.

Means testing carries a huge stigma for many elderly people. They do not like having their finances pored over to see if they qualify for some help from the state.

Children have always been dependent on their parents but have traditionally grown up, in most cases, to aspire to become independent, self-reliant citizens, able to look after themselves. But in the early twenty first century the government had reduced half of the older population to a status similar to that of children, depending on the state to work out how much extra money, if any, they were entitled to be given each week.

The Pension Credit booklet in October 2004 set out the details of a person's savings and investment that would help to determine how much a pensioner might get and ends: "Complicated? Don't worry, we will work it out for you when you call".

The state pension used to be seen as fair: each person regardless of class or income would receive the same fixed sum at a fixed age. It has however been undermined by government intervention causing many older people to feel worry, uncertainty and resentment.

This situation has continued. A report from Age UK published in October 2014 showed that 1.6 million older people were living in poverty, of whom 900,000 were living in severe poverty.

In 2009/2010 around a third (up to 1.6 million) of older people who were entitled to pension credit had not claimed it. Some £5.5bn of state benefit to which pensioners were entitled was not claimed which meant that on average they were missing out on over £1,700 a year (£33 a week).

A system that is so manifestly unjust to those that try and look after themselves and so intrusive into people's private affairs must be condemned. Yet this is the system which the government has imposed. The State can not be trusted.

(d) Position of women

The position of women has been unsatisfactory. Particularly aggrieved are those women who prior to their marriages paid full rate national insurance contributions for many years but did not get any pension from those contributions. The reason that they missed out was the requirement that at least 10 years worth of full contributions must be paid to qualify for the minimum basic pension which was 25% of the full rate.

If they fell short by just a year, they would receive nothing. To get a full pension, they would have needed to work for 39 years, but the 2006 Pension Act reduced this to 30 years.

Some women have suffered however from the fact that their retirement age rose from 60 too quickly.

Ros Altmann, Director General of Saga in a letter to The Times (20/09/11) pointed out that the age at which women were entitled to receive the state pension had been pushed upward more quickly than for men. The reason for this of course was that women had been entitled to receive their pension at a lower age than that for men.

The fact is that in this and in other aspects of social security state control has caused injustice.

(e) Retirement Age

A problem for the nation's finances has been created by the increased expectation of life. When the retirement age was fixed at 65 for men, most were not expected to live many years after that. Now the expectation of life is much greater and people are working longer.

A report from the Office of National Statistics (ONS) published in February 2012 indicated that between 2004 and 2010 the average retirement age increased from 63.8 years to 64.6 years for men and from 61.2 years to 62.3 years for women.

If the present system were to continue, the age at which a pension could be taken would have to be raised significantly unless it is massively subsidised by taxpayers. The government plan was therefore to raise the retirement age to 66 by 2026, to 67 by 2036 and to 68 by 2046.

Pension experts have felt however that increases in life expectancy mean that government is likely to raise the age faster than planned and beyond 68.

In 1981 a man of 65 could expect to live 13 more years while a woman could expect to live 16.7 more years. By 2006 these figures had increased to 17.6 years for men and 20.3 years for women and were expected to reach higher levels by the middle of the century.

Older people are already working hard to supplement their income. The ONS research published in 2012 indicated that 7.3% of all men of or over state pension age continued to work part time and 4.6% full time while 8.9% of women continued to work part time and 3.6% full time.

(f) *No national insurance payments made after retirement age*

After retirement age everyone, whether working or not, is excused payment of national insurance contributions.

According to a report from the Office for National Statistics in 2014, 13% of men over 65 (638,000) were then in paid employment as were 8% of women (453,000) in the same age bracket.

In September 2014 (Sunday Times 7/9/14) the King's Fund proposed that those citizens working beyond the retirement age should pay National Insurance Contributions at 6% , half of what those below retirement age were then paying.

If we had a proper system of insurance in which entitlement depended on past contributions made then people working beyond the retirement age could decide for themselves whether they would like to pay more into the pot from which their pensions would later be drawn. In practice however the N.I. payments made are simply treated as tax and in that case the government can levy what it wants.

(g) *Late Starting Point*

Another minor but significant injustice in the way pension is paid was described by Alison Steed in the Sunday Times (16/11/14).

People expect that when they reach the pensionable age they will begin to be credited with their pension from that date. Apparently however payment is only made from the Monday following a person's birthday. Someone reaching his pensionable age on a Tuesday would not get his pension for 6 days.

This may not be a great injustice but if a private or independent organisation were to promise to pay from your 65th birthday but only did so 6 days later this would be regarded as unacceptable. But on matters of social security the state regards itself as above the scales of justice. According to Alison Steed, moreover, it saves £300m pa by this trick.

(h) The State Second Pension (S2P)

The state second pension has topped up the state pension for employees who made national insurance payments during their working life. Someone who had worked for 40 years earning £40,000 would qualify for a top-up of £105.43 pw as well as the state pension.

The average payout from S2P has been about £26 pw but more than 2 million pensioners have received more than £150 pw through their basic state pension and S2P.

(i) 2013-15. Introduction of a new Pension System

In 2013 the coalition government introduced a white paper setting out a new pension system and in 2014 a Pension Act was passed.

This simplified the system by merging the state basic pension, the second state pension and pension credit into one. The new pension was expected to be paid from April 2016 and to be worth at least £150 pw, rising to £160 pw with inflation by 2017.

Ros Altman, Director General of Saga welcomed the creation of a 'universal pension' which simplified a previously complicated system.

The Department of Work & Pensions (DWP) also plans to link changes in life expectancy to the age at which the pension is paid. This is a reasonable proposition. The plan is to review the pensionable age in 2019 then again in 2026.

Figures obtained by Hargreaves Lansdowne in January 2015 showed that only 45% of pensioners qualifying between 2016 and 2020 would get the full amount.

Some with a private or workplace pension provision are contracted out of some of the state second pension, which is being integrated into the new flat-rate state pension. This means they will receive a lower amount. Others have a gap in their National Insurance contributions.

After April 2017, people will also have to work longer, making 35 years' worth of National Insurance (NI) contributions, rather than the current 30, to qualify for the full pension.

Anyone who has paid NI for less than 10 years will not qualify for the new state pension at all. However, some carers receive NI credits despite being out of the workplace.

"The new state pension will ultimately be a simpler and fairer system. However, in the short term it will be complicated and many people are likely to get less than they may expect" said Tom McPhail, of Hargreaves Lansdowne.

There is also a new provision that someone who delays taking a pension for a year beyond the due date will get a bonus on the pension in all future years.

In many ways these changes are an improvement on the present situation but the basic weaknesses remain. We depend on what the state may provide and this may change and there remains the basic injustice: entitlement does not closely reflect payments in.

The pensioner who emigrates to certain countries such as Australia and Canada is still to receive a pension frozen at the level at which it was initially paid while those who emigrate to Europe get it raised every year.

The state remains unable to be fair in these matters.

2. *Job Seeker's Allowance*

A second possibility of need arises when fit and able people do not have the opportunity of employment on which to rely for their main income. The state has accepted responsibility for ensuring that such people receive 'unemployment benefit' or, as it is now known, 'Jobseeker's Allowance'. Before this is given however, the means of the jobseeker has to be assessed and deductions may be made to take account of other income. The full allowance for 2014 was £72 pw (£57 for under 25's), increased to £73.10 (£57.90 for under 25's) in 2015. This would be the same for someone who had been working for 30 years (who really needs much more) as it would be for a young person who had never worked.

In June 2015 the DWP published conditions which only someone with considerable skill and knowledge could be expected to work out. The claimant, for instance, must have worked for 26 weeks in one of the two previous tax years and have paid class I National Insurance Contributions or received NI credits in both of these tax years that would amount to 50 times the lower earning limits. The DWP clearly wishes to have rules which only a few ordinary people are able to understand.

Problems with the system.

A problem arises when someone on Job Seeker's Allowance has the chance to earn a few pounds by part-time working. If this is declared then benefit is reduced. So this person may turn up once a week for cash and work part-time for undeclared income on other days.

Some people receiving the benefit may have the opportunity for full-time work for a short period but may be afraid that if they lose this job it will take time for the benefit to get restored. So they may be tempted either to turn down the work or to do it and carry on drawing benefit.

Dr. Len May, in a letter to the Independent (12/08/03) made the position clear: "To the best of my knowledge it is not illegal to work whilst claiming benefit. What is illegal is to fail to declare that income to the Employment Services so that it can be deducted from benefit payments. Honest claimants who find short periods of work with reputable employers and declare their earnings can find that the deductions from benefits are made immediately but they do not receive their pay for two or more weeks. It can also be difficult to re-establish an entitlement to benefit once the work ceases and there is always a delay before benefits are paid again. Benefit claimants are unlikely to have the resources to tide them over during such periods. In the circumstances should we be entirely surprised that a few people succumb to the temptation to be dishonest?" This benefit may both undermine personal integrity and defraud the state.

Others may actually find the benefit sufficient for their needs, particularly if they live with working members of their family with whom they have meals. Within a marriage or other partnership, one person may work and the other may choose not to work – but claim benefit nonetheless.

In December 2006, at a time of generally high unemployment, with 600,000 vacancies and an estimated 500,000 Eastern European workers in the UK there were nevertheless 950,000 British people receiving Jobseeker's Allowance (Times 18/12/06); 100,000 of these had been Job Seeker's Allowance claimants for at least 6 of the previous 7 years while 70% of new claimants had claimed before.

There has thus been a state of war going on between the state which wants its payments to go to those who need it and certain sections of the population who try and milk the system. In the early 21st century the state appears to be winning the war. According to national statistics published in November 2006, fraud in Jobseeker's allowance fell from £70m in the year to September 2004 to £40m in the year to September 2005. It is sad that £40m is so easily wasted but even more sad that the benefits system leads to conflict.

According to the Sunday Times (25/04/10), former Trade Minister Lord Jones suggested that unemployed young people who refused to look for a job should be starved back to work.

A BBC Panorama documentary in April 2010 featured two men from Swindon. One told Jones that he and his girlfriend get roughly £15-£16,000 a year based on Jobseeker's Allowance and Housing Benefit. The man said that there was "no reason for them to look for work".

While looking for a job, claimants should carry out community work e.g. cleaning toilets said Lord Jones. He believed anyone who has refused 3 offers of a job should lose the dole, be put in a hostel and given subsidence rations.

As Jamie McGuinness reported in the Times (11/07/10), official figures in May 2010 showed that more than 7,000 vacancies in job centres had been advertised for at least 6 months. Of those, 94 had been advertised for a year or more and 48 for at least two years.

In 2010, Teignbridge in Devon had more job vacancies advertised for 9-12 months than any other local authority area in Britain. The high number of elderly people in the area had brought strong demand for care workers, jobs that were often difficult to fill. Yet the town had 1,451 people claiming Jobseeker's Allowance.

In Newton Abbot, the biggest town in the area covered by the local authority, the unemployment rate was 4.3%. Yet Barbara Byrne, manager at Coombeswood nursing home in Kingsteignton, Newton Abbot said she had a job for an apprentice care assistant that had been available for more than a year and she had just filled a second post. She said many locals who enquired about jobs would rather stay on the dole and those from eastern Europe who used to fill low-skilled posts had gone home.

It is therefore easy to conclude that some people would rather stay on benefits than work in care homes or call centres or perform other low-skilled roles.

In 2010, an unemployed 24 year old man living in a one bedroom council flat in Newton Abbot with his jobless girlfriend and their child could expect £51.85 pw in Jobseeker's Allowance, £54.67 in Child Tax Credits and £60 in Housing Benefit, a total of more than £160, not including his girlfriend's benefits. A typical 35 hour week at the nursing home would bring only an extra £50.

Chris Grayling Employment Minister at the time commented "The fact that these jobs are advertised for a long period shows the current welfare system is not working. After a decade of throwing money at the problem, there are still 5 million people out of work, living on benefits".

Sanctions

It is not surprising therefore that the state seeks to impose sanctions on those for whom work is available but who choose not to take it. In April 2001 the government made clear that anyone under 50 who refused a job, training or voluntary work would (unless a single parent or disabled) face cuts in benefits.

Later the government intervened to ensure that both partners in a childless couple could not receive the allowance unless both were ready to accept a job or training.

John Hutton, then Work and Pensions Secretary, in a speech to the IPPR in December 2006 voiced the widely held concern about those who claimed the benefit but had no big physical or health barriers to working and lived in areas where there was no shortage of vacancies. His view was that if the cycle of benefit dependency was to be broken in this group then consideration should be given to expecting something in return for the help provided. For those who refused to take steps to get back into the labour market or to get involved in programmes that could increase the prospect of getting a job, "there should" he said "be consequences, including less benefit or no benefit at all".

The coalition government formed in 2010 continued the war against those who could work but failed to do so.

In 2011 it introduced a 'mandatory work activity' for some 10,000 claimants who were told that if they were to receive benefits they must work unpaid for 4 weeks. If they did not do so then their benefit would not be paid. According to the Sunday Times (08/01/12) the response was revealing: 20% of the claimants refused the offer while another 30% did not turn up for the work.

Following this tougher approach from the government, more than 580,000 unemployed people claiming Jobseeker's Allowance lost benefit.

Figures from the Department of Work and Pensions (DWP) released in November 2013 showed an 11% rise in penalties for failing to turn up for a Jobcentre appointment "with no good reason", failing to show that they had searched for a job or refusing to take work once it was offered.

Claimants were docked a minimum of four weeks' benefits for a first offence. The maximum sanction for repeat offenders is three years.

The most common reason for a Jobseeker's Allowance sanction (36%) was a failure to look for work; 30% were sanctioned for failing to participate in employment programmes and 20% for missing a Jobseeker meeting. The figures however showed that the number of most severe sanctions had reduced in 2013, almost halving compared with 2012.

The DWP stated that claimants were much more likely to face sanctions for failing to look for a job under the new rules. Esther McVey, then Minister for Employment, said the Government had always been clear that in return for claiming unemployment benefits jobseekers had a responsibility to do everything they could to get back to work. "We are ending the something for nothing culture" she said.

DWP figures published in March 2014 showed that more than 900,000 JSA claimants were sanctioned between April 2013 and March 2014. More than half of these were aged under 30; 370,162 were aged 18-24 and 145,708 were 25-29. As explained in a File on Four broadcast on Radio 4 (20/1/15) these sanctions imposed on the jobless have caused real hardship to many, forcing them to turn to food banks for their sustenance.

Ed Milliband interviewed in June 2014 said that if he became Prime Minister he would end entitlement to adult out-of-work benefits for 18 – 21 year olds with no qualifications. Instead, he said, they would get a youth allowance if they agreed to undertake vocational training at AS level or the equivalent. At the moment, they are prevented by benefit rules from training while looking for work.

The new allowance was expected to be paid at the same level as that given to under-25s on Jobseeker's Allowance. But it would be means tested so those with a family income of more than £42,000 a year would not be entitled to the new allowance. The policy was expected to affect about 100,000 young people.

So Labour as well as Conservative politicians are ready to join the attack on the young jobless. Meanwhile, the whole process of paying out money to the unemployed entails that a vast amount of money is spent on the bureaucracy of civil servants to ensure that no state money is wasted.

According to DWP statistics published in November 2014 there were 1,444,411 sanctions applied to JSA claimants between 22nd October 2012 and June 2014. Of these 810,364 were low level sanctions; 511,884 were intermediate level sanctions and 121,105 were high level sanctions. In addition, the statistics showed that 379,887 decisions were reviewed (and in 190,746 cases the decision was overturned), while 39,009 were appealed – and in 7,832 cases the decision was overturned.

In the same month (November 2014) the Work and Pensions Committee of the House of Commons launched an enquiry into the government's sanction policy. They would try and find out whether there was evidence that the sanction policy really worked and whether it really did encourage claimants to engage more actively in job seeking and what impact it had on the claimants themselves. But what is really wrong is a benefits system in which the state goes to war against its own people whom it should be protecting.

To blame the people who could work but don't misses the point. The fault lies in a benefit system which makes it so easy for people to take money from the state. The system damages most the people who otherwise would be making a useful contribution to society. Those damaged most are the young who may well feel they are better off with a weekly cash hand-out than they would be working or training.

How much better it would be if the state was not involved and people could secure income from their own financial resources. How this could be done is explained in Part II of this book.

Providing opportunities for work, training and education.

A second and more commendable strand in government policy is the provision of opportunities for work, training and education.

In 2012 the coalition government introduced a work programme in which unemployed people needing an income were expected to enrol. DWP statistics published on 18th September 2014 showed that in the year ending on 30th June 2014, one in eight of those on the programme had secured a job. One in five of those aged 18 to 24 had spent at least 6 months in work in the 12 month period, while one in six of those aged over 24 had done so.

The government had earlier announced plans to limit JobSeeker's Allowance for 18 to 21 year olds to 6 months after which they must do community work if they were to claim benefits.

In February 2015 however Mr Cameron scrapped this idea and insisted that young people should be immediately put into community work if they wanted to claim benefit. They should undertake at least 30 hours community work a week and spend 10 hours looking for jobs. Anyone required to undertake community work would receive a "youth allowance" equivalent in value to the Jobseeker's Allowance.

One strange thing about the work programme is that it is controlled nationally and through Job Centres, not by local councils.

Local authorities themselves feel it would be right for them to take more responsibility. On 31st March 2015 the Local Government Association set out proposals for the government to devolve to them at least £15 bn worth of employment and skills funding which would enable them to secure long-term employment for many more people.

The DWP then found out that most of the unemployed 18-12 year olds were deficient in their level of general education especially in literacy and numeracy. This made it hard for them to do a job which required such ability. In |January 2015 it issued new guidance on the work skills pilot scheme for JSA claimants aged 18-21. This was designed to assist 18-21 year old JSA claimants to improve their chances of obtaining employment by supporting them to develop their English and Maths skills (Phase One) or to undertake skills training or work-related activity, such as work experience (Phase Two).

The lower level of general education is however the predictable result of the idiotic policy which the government has imposed on schools and pupils since the end of the twentieth century. What the state should do is to ask a well qualified committee to set out what knowledge, understanding and skills young people should have by 15 and 17 say. They would then be examined on their capacity in these areas and awarded grades as appropriate. Of course students should after a certain age be able to specialise in some subjects as well but their general education should come first.

But the government has failed to set up any system for examination for general education after 11. Instead pupils are assessed on their ability in specialist subjects and schools graded on the results of their pupils who get good marks in 5 specialist subjects at GCSE.

It is easy then for students to assume that doing well in 5 or 6 subjects is what matters, not their general education. If moreover 10% of the year group are not thought likely to do well in the subjects they take then teachers will be far less interested in their education than they are for those who might, with hard work and encouragement, reach an acceptable standard.

Only if this unhelpful system is changed will all young people be well educated.

3. Income Support

If other sources of income, whether state provided or not, are insufficient then a person may claim Income Support (formerly Supplementary Benefit). Problems however arise. One family with no or little other income receives Income Support to bring their income up to, say, £180 pw. A second family has one parent in a full-time job earning £180 pw. So both families will ask themselves "what's the point of working?" Moreover, if they work they have to pay out more for clothes, travel and other ordinary costs.

Furthermore, once people have Income Support they may qualify for other benefits such as free school meals for their children. This encourages dishonesty since those on Income Support will be tempted to conceal other sources of income that they have.

One particularly damaging use of income support is to support lone parents. This is dealt with in section 6 (c) below.

The cost of the benefit in 2015/16 was £2.5 bn according to H.M.Treasury figures published in the Times (9/3/15) but the government hopes to reduce it to £2.3 bn in 2020/21.

4. Housing Benefit

During and after the Second World War rents were controlled but they were partially decontrolled in the late twentieth century in an effort to create a freer market in rented housing and to make more privately owned premises available. This sometimes led to a considerable rise in rents which for many were unaffordable.

Housing benefit was introduced to help those who could not afford to pay (although some other tenants continued to live in houses with controlled or regulated rent). According to Treasury figures published in the Times (9/7/15) the cost to the government in 2015/16 was £23.7 bn.

Local authorities have been responsible for paying housing benefit according to rules set by central government. They subsequently recover this from the government.

The rules became increasingly complex. Eligibility for benefit depended not only on earned income but also on other benefits and other sources of income such as an occupational pension. It also depended on family responsibilities and necessary outgoings. The level of benefits depended on the relationship between the balance of income and a person's 'applicable amount' which was what the government decreed was needed to live on each week. If the income balance was less than or equal to this 'applicable amount' then the maximum housing benefit should be awarded unless those affected had investment income. In that case the council worked out what additional income arose from these savings and this "tariff" income, as it was termed, was added to a person's assumed income balance and thus reduced housing benefit payable. Those who had savings above a certain sum did not qualify for benefit at all.

Council house tenants have had housing benefit credited to their rent account. Private or housing association tenants have had their benefit paid to them unless it was agreed that it should be paid direct to the private landlord or housing association.

The most obvious criticism of this procedure is its complexity. There were many circumstances in addition to those mentioned above that the council official had to consider before awarding a benefit. Each application must be dealt with individually.

Again, circumstances may change: a tenant may get a job, have a child, receive an inheritance, face a rental increase for instance – the entitlement to benefit may change and so the matter must be referred to the council. As a result of this complexity the benefit is costly to administer. It is, moreover, open to fraud.

Someone on Income Support for instance might find somewhere to rent a room and the Council would provide housing benefit to cover all or part of the rent but not the cost of heating and other services. Sometimes the tenant could stay more cheaply with family or friends in which case the housing benefit payment would be either totally or partly unnecessary. An unemployed young man of 20 living with his parents could move out to rent a room of his own – the council will pay it all, he cheerfully tells his prospective landlord. Landlords may still pretend to be renting a room to a person even if that person has been sleeping elsewhere.

According to figures issued by the Department of Work and Pensions in February 2007 (Times 13/02/07) £770m was overpaid in 2005/06, of which £140m was due to fraud, £190m to official error and £440m to customer error. In 2010 it was found that there were 3,400 families receiving housing benefit of £26,000 p.a. or more.

The most obvious examples of large benefit payments are to be found in London. Nicola Woodcock in the Times (25/5/15) gives examples of cases originally published in the Mail on Sunday. She reveals that ten families have claimed more than £400,000 in housing benefit in two London boroughs. In Westminster, nine claimants have been paid more than £400,000 and a family living in a four bedroom house in Kensington and Chelsea have received £476,635 since 2006.

The payments are high because of the price of accommodating families in prime areas of London. One family of three, living in a flat, has been paid the equivalent of £46,000 a year in housing benefit for 11 years. The claimant and the two children, aged 11 and 12, are living in a property with five bedrooms and three bathrooms. They have been paid more than £515,400 since 2004. Another family receives £695 a week to live in a postcode covering South Kensington and Knightsbridge.

Many councils have waiting lists of families needing to move into bigger properties but who are housed in temporary accommodation or flats that are too small.

Mark Field, the Conservative MP for Cities of London & Westminster, told the newspaper: "If these are people who aren't in work and are never going to be in paid employment, it doesn't make much sense that they're housed in central London, particularly when there are hundreds of thousands of people coming to work in my constituency every day and who would love to live in central London, but rents are so high they can't afford to do so."

In 2004, a report predicted that the cost of housing benefit would rise from £17 bn a year in 2008 to £27 bn by 2018, by which time 1.2 million people would be claiming the subsidy. Information such as this is what justifies the use of the term 'crazy' to describe the British benefit system.

What is really needed is a new housing policy which would make it possible for almost anyone to rent a home. Politicians however concentrate on cutting the cost of the benefit.

The coalition government, from 2010, was determined to reduce the cost of housing benefit. In March 2012 its Welfare Reform Act ruled that from 2013 housing benefit payments for claimants of working age would be related to the size of property, with payment reduced for those "under-occupying".

The government planned that, from October 2013, housing benefit for those of working age would gradually be swallowed up and replaced by a housing element within the new Universal Credit (and Pension Credit for those of retirement age). Claims would mostly be made and managed online and payments made on a monthly basis. Vulnerable tenants might still be able to have the housing elements of Universal Credit paid directly to their landlord. This reform was to some extent implemented as planned in 2013. The government imposed a cap on the amount which an individual could receive. Those with a spare room were told to move to a smaller house if they were to receive benefit. This had most effect in London where the new reforms were first introduced.

According to Jill Sherman in the Times (24/05/13) children had to spend up to four hours a day commuting to school as nearly 600 families had been forced out of London due to a shortage of cheap accommodation.

According to Shelter the housing benefit cap forced an increasing number of families to face a choice between changing schools or travelling long distances. Some London authorities moved families as far away as Devon and Manchester. Shelter found that 11,513 homeless households had been placed in temporary housing outside their home borough.

Some councils were believed to be acting in breach of the Housing Act 1996, which says that suitable accommodation should be found taking account of jobs and schools. Bed and breakfast is an alternative. Hammersmith and Fulham council spent £859,863 on 365 families in bed and breakfast.

The Times in its leading article (16/07/13) commented that this policy would force thousands of people out of their homes and that this would impose on the government a moral obligation - in addition to many practical ones – to engineer a rapid, large scale increase in the supply of low-cost housing.

Initially some 40,000 households were affected by the cap, more than half of them in Greater London. This is no surprise, given soaring London rents and the rise in housing benefit to help to pay them for families without an adult in work.

The Bedroom Tax

The aspect of government policy which aroused most criticism was the so-called 'bedroom tax'. If householders receiving housing benefit had a spare room they were told that if they were to receive housing benefit they must move to a smaller home without a spare room.

Householders who kept a spare room for family members who lived away at some distance were no longer able to ask them to stay in this spare room when they made a visit.

A special problem was created for separated families where the parents shared custody. The mother needed a spare room for the children when they stayed with her. The father needed the room for when they stayed with him.

In 2012 the Housing Benefit regulations were amended to reduce the benefit payable to whichever parents had secondary responsibility. But there are cases where custody is shared equally. In these cases each received housing benefit. The children alternated between living with each parent, spending approximately half their time with each and having their own bedroom at each premises. This left the authorities in some doubt as to what to do and in some cases the local authority made discretionary housing payments (DHP) to the parent without prime responsibility.

According to statistics published by the DWP in February 2014, nearly half a million claimants were affected by the bedroom tax in November 2013.

They showed that it was applied to 498,174 claimants with an average housing benefit reduction of £14.40 per week. They also showed a wide regional variation in the average reduction, ranging from £20.12 in London to £11.32 in Scotland.

The impact of the first 8 months following the implementation of this bedroom tax was set out in a report published on 14th July 2014 (Evaluation of the removal of the spare room subsidy – interim report). This research showed that 4.5 per cent of affected claimants were reported by landlords to have downsized within the social sector within the first six months of implementation while 59 per cent of tenants affected by the bedroom tax had failed to make up the shortfall in rent. The report also showed that not all disabled people had been awarded discretionary housing payments (DHP's).

More than half (56.1%) of bedroom tax claimants surveyed who had not applied for DHP said they were unaware of it, these being the individuals likely to report difficulties paying rent. 18.1% said they looked to earn more through employment related income as a result of the bedroom tax.

According to a National Housing Federation (NHF) report published on 8th January 2015, two thirds of housing association tenants affected by the bedroom tax were finding it hard to pay their rent. The NHF found that whist the numbers of tenants affected by the bedroom tax who were in arrears had fallen since autumn 2013, for those who were in arrears, their situation had worsened, with almost two-thirds of currently affected tenants in arrears in that position due to a failure to pay the bedroom tax, compared to an estimated 52 per cent in autumn 2013. Two thirds of affected tenants (67 per cent) reported they were finding it difficult to afford to pay their rent, compared to less than a third of non-affected tenants (31 per cent).

In a letter to the Times (14/8/14) the Reverend Paul Nicholson, for 'Taxpayers against Poverty' wrote that in February 2013 there were 5.1 million claimants of housing benefit in the UK. Some were totally dependent on that benefit to keep a roof over their heads. Come April 2013 and the poorest large families (£26,000 annual limit) and single people (spare room supplement) had their housing benefit cut, leaving rent unpaid and eviction threatening.

"Low paid single people, widows and widowers, around 50 to 60 years old, becoming ill or unemployed for the first time in a long, working, tax-paying life could no longer depend on the rest of us to keep them in their family home among vital community support. The policy is to force them to move to make a better use of affordable social housing. Large families with young children suffer the same fate just because they happened to be large on April 6ᵗʰ 2013.

A very small minority of benefit claimants might be dependent on benefits to such an extent that it is corrosive to the well-being of individuals. Most need them but wish they did not. Yet all are publicly branded and their incomes reduced, even though the fault lies with the lack of any governmental policy to provide enough affordable housing for many decades. We must accept that the bedroom tax has caused great difficulty to some of our poorer families."

On the 16ᵗʰ March 2015 the Guardian published an article based on a report from the Journal of Public Health detailing the effect of the bedroom tax in the deprived ward of Walker in Newcastle. This found that worries around debt, rent arrears and the prospect of being forced to move from their family home produced a sense of "hopelessness verging on desperation." People reported being trapped in a "vicious cycle" of loneliness and isolation; they could often no longer afford to go to the pub or café, or even carry out family roles such as grandparenting.

Contrary to the government's assertion when the policy was introduced that it would have no negative impact on health and well being, the study concluded that the bedroom tax had "increased poverty and had broad-ranging adverse effects on health, well being and social relationships."

Dr Wendy Ross, a GP in Walker for 23 years, agreed it was difficult to isolate the bedroom tax as a sole cause. But patients often reported the bedroom tax as the cause of stress. "One middle-aged lady who has lived in Walker all her life presented with minor mental health problems and anxiety because she'd been hit by the bedroom tax and had been offered a smaller house in Sunderland (at least 15 miles away)."

Walker resident Susan Bell, 59, told the Guardian of the pressure that the bedroom tax placed on her before she became one of the few people to be downsized to a smaller home in her neighbourhood. "It was all stress. They put me on blood pressure tablets." Joyce McCarty, deputy leader of Newcastle City Council, told the Guardian the bedroom tax had created problems where none existed. There were no families in Newcastle living in overcrowded conditions, no social housing shortage and no homelessness – in fact, it now had to manage a surfeit of empty larger properties because families would not move into bigger houses in case they too became subject to the bedroom tax.

One result of this pressure on housing is that some people are left homeless. According to research by Crisis and the Joseph Rowntree Foundation published in December 2013 sleeping rough had risen by 6 per cent in England and 13 per cent in London. In those two years homelessness in the capital rose by more than 60 per cent. "Homelessness is the tragic consequence of failures in our housing system and carries enormous cost for both the people facing destitution and society as a whole", said Julia Unwin, the chief executive of the Joseph Rowntree Foundation. "We need to address the underlying causes of homelessness urgently."

In his 2015 Budget the Chancellor of the Exchequer announced that housing benefit would not be paid to unemployed young people aged 18 to 21 John Sparkes, chief executive of the Crisis charity, said the move could increase homelessness and cost the taxpayer more than they save. "We are particularly worried about cuts to housing benefit for 18-21s" he said.

"Under 25s already make up a third of homeless people and there is a real danger these changes could make things even worse."

It is alleged, understandably, that cuts in housing benefit in 2013 have made the situation worse. There had been many attacks on the spare bedroom tax, but why should society subsidise such housing?

What should happen is that there should be enough accommodation available for rent and the people that need a house must have enough money to meet the cost without the need for housing benefit or other government intervention. How this might be achieved is described later. Meanwhile there simply have not been enough houses being built, a little more than 100,000 a year in 2012 compared to 300,000 in the 1950's. Yet Britain's population is rising fast thanks partially to increased immigration and increased numbers of children being born but also because of the increased expectation of life and to many older people living alone because of separation from their partner.

For most aspects of social security the state must take the blame for making such a mess of it. When it comes to housing, the capitalist system must share the blame. There is inadequate low cost housing partly because building firms like to build attractive houses that will sell well not inexpensive housing for the poor. How this can be tackled is set out in the last few pages of Part II.

5. Council Tax Benefit/Support

The Council Tax Benefit, now known as Council Tax Support, is administered by local councils to help poor householders who, on the basis of means testing, are adjudged to be deserving of financial help. This can be particularly important for older people who no longer work but still live in a large house. An elderly gentleman rang his local council to ask to be sent details of how such a benefit would be worked out. The official replied that he did not have such details available as they were in various

Acts of Parliament but that if he could be told the caller's income and other financial details, he would work out whether the gentleman calling qualified for council tax benefit and, if so, for how much. The elderly gentleman then said that he did not wish to talk about his income: all he wanted was to be sent a copy of the rules applicable so that he could work out for himself whether or not he qualified and, if so, for how much. Then he would be happy to submit the figures for the officials to check – but not until he had seen the rules and worked it out for himself. The official was adamant: the caller should give his income and he, the official, would work it out but he could not agree to send a statement of how this would be done. It is not surprising that many pensioners, in particular, fail to apply for council tax benefits. The DWP stated in January 2005 that as few as 65% of those eligible applied for the benefit, saving the government up to £1.2 billion a year. The DWP admitted that the number of pensioners who had applied for council tax benefits had fallen by up to 10% between 1997 and 2004.

The coalition government formed in 2010 initiated a radical change in the way council tax benefit would be administered. Previously the councils had administered the scheme but central government had met the cost. From April 2013 however, councils were expected not only to pay out the benefit but also to meet the cost themselves – although a Transition Fund was established from which financial help (of £100m) could be given to councils in the first year.

In January 2014 the Local Government Association (LGA) warned that if central government cuts were passed on to residents, then local councils could have £1 billion less for council tax support between 2013/14 and 2015/16.

Cllr Sharon Taylor, Chair of the LGA's Finance Panel, explained the position of councils. "Councils are now facing an impossible dilemma between making bigger reductions to local service like repairing the roads, collecting the bins and looking after the elderly or asking those on the lowest incomes to pay more council tax.

When government handed councils the responsibility for administering council tax support, it cut hundreds of millions in funding for it. The shortfall between the money councils receive to fund council tax support and the money we would need to protect those on low incomes is going to get bigger and is likely to reach £1 bn by 2016. At the same time, councils are tackling the biggest cuts in living memory and cannot afford to meet the shortfall.

Councils have been forced to choose between asking working-aged claimants to pay more tax or taking much-needed money away from other services. Protecting the most vulnerable and needy members of society is a priority for councils, but we cannot protect those on the lowest incomes when government is cutting funding and taking some of the decisions about who receives this benefit out of our hands."

In July 2014, the New Policy Initiative, using new Department for Communities and Local Government statistics, showed that whilst more than £1 bn extra council tax was collected in England in 2013/14, in-year arrears increased by £145 million – up more than 20 per cent on the previous year. In November 2014 the Audit Commission published figures showing that the total council tax arrears owed to individual councils at the end of March 2014 ranged from £11.1m to £105.2m.

The Local Government Association (LGA) commented that the 'consequence of government cutting funding for council tax support had left local authorities with little option but to reduce discounts for people on low incomes, some of whom have found it a struggle to pay'.

In January 2015 the LGA warned that from April 2015 more than two million families would face higher council tax (Times 6/1/15). The association predicted that tens of thousands of new families would forego their discount partially or entirely, adding hundreds of pounds to their annual bill. In addition, up to 2.4 million families who have seen their discount drop in the past two years could have to pay more.

An LGA report showed that in 244 council areas all households had to pay at least some council tax regardless of income – 15 more than in 2013-14. One in seven councils said they definitely planned to change their discount scheme and for the following year only 27 per cent said they would be able to maintain the existing subsidies. The LGA called on the next government to fund council tax support at the same level as before April 2013. Some councils were giving discount on council tax to low income households while other councils were not. Some councils give a bigger discount than others. Council tax benefit is therefore grossly unfair.

Commenting on these findings, Chair of the LGA David Sparks said that as a result of government cuts, councils would need to find £1bn by 2016 to protect discounts for those on low incomes. At a time when local government was already tackling £20bn worth of cuts, this was a stretch too far.

In April 2015 New Policy Initiative published a report on council tax support which showed that from April 2015, 250 councils required all residents to pay some council tax regardless of income, up from 229 in 2013/14. 2.3m low income families were adversely affected by the April 2013 change from council tax benefit (CTB) to locally devised council tax support (CTS) schemes.

In its third year (2015/16) 2.3m low income families have been adversely affected by the change from CTB to CTS – on average they have had to pay £167 more council tax in 2015/2016 than they did under the former CTB system. From April 2015, 250 councils require all residents to pay some council tax regardless of income, up from 229 in 2013/14 – the range of these 'minimum payments' is between 5 and 30 per cent of council tax liability. Compared to under the former CTB system, in 2015/16 590,000 families have to pay £200 more per year in council tax as a result of 'minimum payments', up from 450,000 in 2013/14.

The difficulties created by having council tax support cut was illustrated in an article by Dawn Foster in the Guardian (2/4/15). She tells the story of Eve and her three children.

Eve's financial position worsened when her council tax support was cut after April 2013. Eve became one of millions suddenly liable for council tax payments, when previously she would have been exempt due to poverty. Once you miss a payment, within 14 days you can find yourself in court, as Eve did, with a fifth of her income confiscated each month. Then the bailiffs arrived. In a rented, furnished flat, there was nothing to take, but the visits made her contemplate suicide.

The scope of the cuts to council tax support were extreme: more than 2.3 million families have lost out and in the first six months of the policy, almost half a million people were issued court summons for arrears.

More than 2.3 million families lost their council tax support.

In April 2015, 250,000 low-income families would see their council tax payments increase substantially because they live in one of the 27 areas that were raising or introducing the minimum payment. Families were expected to pay between 5% and 30% of their total council tax liability – what sounds like a small sum cuts drastically into the day-to-day budgets of people already in entrenched poverty.

Once a payment is missed, the costs mount quickly and the situation can escalate. Council tax debt carries a threat of imprisonment if unpaid, a fact that people in the courtrooms are told repeatedly A few missed payments and suddenly a court summons lands on your doormat and your arrears are deducted automatically from your benefits, along with court fees and administrative costs. The debts pile up and you're poorer that ever.

The Children's Society has raised concerns that bailiff visits as a result of council tax debt are adversely affecting children's mental health and well being. Most bailiff visits occur when children are at home and many of them have come to associate the knock at the door with their parents' fear.

The fact that having children leaves you vulnerable to greater financial difficulty and council tax arrears usually result in the local authority demanding the full annual payment compounds the debt.

Council tax may seem a sensible way to raise money for the government levied as it is on the householder. A problem arises because councils have agreed to some households having allowances to reduce the tax they pay. Councils have had to make decisions as to which householders should get this allowance and as indicated in the first paragraph in this section, they do not publicise the way in which they do so.

It would of course be much simpler if it was the house owner who paid council tax not the tenant even when the house is owned by the council or by a housing association. Many tenants in certain areas struggle to make ends meet and many are therefore given reductions in the council tax they have to pay. But this happens in a way which disregards justice. Someone in one town gets a reduction of £x while someone in another town living in precisely the same circumstances gets no reduction.

This uncertain benefit must be scrapped with all the others and the arrangements to be made for properties to be charged council tax must be radically changed.

6. Child support and parental benefit

(a) Child Benefit

Payments for children are a well established non means tested way of helping parents bring up children. Since the future of society depends on today's children this is a reasonable way of ensuring that parents have the resources they need to bring them up well. Unlike most other benefits, child benefit is basically right.

One long standing problem however is the fact that such payments are made in cash, usually to the mother, and some well-off parents may simply give the money to their children. Research by Warwick University reported in the Sunday Times (03/09/06) showed however that most parents spent it on themselves. Such payments moreover are not taxed: the millionaire receives these payments in full.

At least, however, these payments were the same for all; there was no having to work out the income of all parents to determine the sum paid. In 1998 however, the all-party Commons Education Select Committee recommended and the government subsequently accepted that child benefit should be scrapped for 16 to 19 year olds and replaced by cash handouts for those still in education. All teenagers over 15 in full-time education would be eligible for means-tested payments. Any child whose parents earned more than a specified sum would not qualify but all other youngsters, in private or state schools or further education colleges would receive these payments. It was hoped that this financial award would persuade more young people to stay at school. This Educational Maintenance Allowance was abolished by the coalition government in 2010.

By 2010 Child Benefit was costing the government £11.3 billion of which £4.8 billion (43%) was paid out to those earning more than the national average. There was some pressure on the coalition government formed in

2010 to reduce this. In 2012 the government decided to reduce child benefit payments to high earners.

With effect from 7th January 2013, the high income benefit charge has been applied by HMRC when a taxpayer's or their partner's income is more than £50,000 in a tax year – for those with income of more than £60,000, the tax charge is 100 per cent of the amount of child benefit, whilst, if income is between £50,000 and £60,000, the charge has been gradually increased to 100 per cent of the child benefit.

In other words, there is now means-testing for child benefit. Means testing however always causes unfairness and a much greater cost in administration. If you earn more than the specified sum you get no child benefit for your children but the family next door earns just a bit less than you do so they still get child benefit for their three children. This is grossly unfair.

In January 2014 a government report, published by the Guardian, showed that one in ten of those affected by the high income child benefit charge, that was introduced on 7th January 2013, had yet to register with HMRC. This created additional cost in administration.

How much simpler and juster it would be if those having to pay 40% in tax would be taxed on their child benefit.

Early in 2015 the Institute of Fiscal Studies (IFS) warned that hundreds of thousands of parents would lose their child benefit and face higher taxes in the coming years as rising wages drag them above the welfare threshold.

The first child clearly has a bigger financial impact on parents and it is right for society to help with the provision of care. Indeed this is reflected in the arrangement currently in place. In 2014 child benefit of £20-50 pw was paid for the oldest child and £13-55 pw for any additional children.

In July 2014 the Policy Exchange think tank proposed that payments should be reduced for each child after the first and there should be no benefit for any child born after the fourth with effect from April 2016. A YouGov poll, which surveyed 2,095 British adults, found that 67 per cent thought that people who had four children should not receive extra child benefit if they had a fifth. Policy Exchange reaffirmed this policy in February 2015, claiming that this would save £1 bn over 5 years.

In 2015-16 according to Treasury figures published in the Times (9/7/15) child benefit still cost £11.5 bn, somewhat more than in 2010.

On the 2nd June 2015, Sam Coates in the Times reported that there had been a battle in the cabinet as some ministers including Ian Duncan-Smith were expecting to cut back on child benefit.

At the start of the 2015 campaign, Mr Osborne appeared to keep the Tories' options open, refusing to rule out plans to wrap the handout into universal credit which would save about £4.5 billion.

A week before polling day, Mr Cameron promised in front of the camera that he would protect child benefit in its current form for five years. That commitment is now unbreakable.

At the lower income level there is some suspicion that some parents – or perhaps just mothers – use children as a money maker, going on sometimes to have ten or more.

A Channel 5 programme on benefits in January 2015 followed three households each containing 7 children. The mother of course receives child benefit for them all but it also means that they have to live in large houses with room for all the children. To rent such houses may cost a sizeable sum which the state pays through housing benefit.

The view that used to be taken was that both parents together should take full responsibility for the children. If the mother looks after them the father should work to provide an income - although the state has an interest in future citizens and rightly contributes. Yet now many fathers do not contribute much for the upkeep of their children.

How people may thrive with the help of child benefit as well as other benefits was illustrated by Gabriella Swerling in the Times (27/1/15) – Cheryl Prudha, 32, a pregnant mother with 11 children, took her family on overseas holidays while claiming £38,000 a year in benefits; she claimed the money in child allowances, tax credits and housing benefit with her husband Robert. She has alleged that Mr Prudham, who has fathered her five youngest children, has left her several times during their six-year relationship. Mrs Prudham, who lives in a five bedroom council house in Gravesend, Kent, had her first son, George, when she was 17. She met Mr Prudham in March 2009. The couple both work 20 hours a week as carers for the elderly. She claims £38,000 of tax credits and benefits a year on top of this.

There has also been concern that the British government, under EU rules, has to pay child benefit for the children of those eastern Europeans when working in Britain even though they and usually the mother live in a country on the European mainland. Treasury figures published in 2014 showed that in 2013 22,093 of the children who were benefiting were Poles.

David Cameron commented in May 2014 "If you travel and work from another European country into Britain, you can then claim child benefit and other benefits for your family back at home even though actually they're not living in the UK and going to UK schools and all the rest of it." Tougher measures are necessary to reduce the unfairness.

Child benefit has come under attack from some quarters. K. Brown from Edinburgh in a letter to the Times (25/09/10) argued that "It is a matter of choice to have children and it should not be undertaken lightly; quite different from being old or disabled, where there is no choice, and society should do all it can to protect these groups. Child benefit is the single most pernicious payment in the British system. It would be unfair to take it away from those already with children so I suggest that it be scrapped for children born more than a year from now and phased out for existing claimants over a five year period."

Not many would take this view. Looking after our children is vital to the quality of the next generation. However it would not be unreasonable to support only the first 3 or 4 children.

(b) Maternity Benefit

The government also makes a payment to mothers who would normally work but need time at home to have a baby. Traditionally 6 months has been allowed but the Blair government extended this to 9 months from April 2007 and to 12 months from 2009. By 2015-16 this cost £2.3 bn according to Treasury figures published in the Times (9/7/15).

If the mother-to-be has been employed by a company or other institution at least 20 weeks before the baby is due to be born, she is entitled to statutory maternity pay, which is paid by the company. If not, she must claim from the benefits agency. If the employer is required to pay her, she is entitled to 90% of her normal salary for the first six weeks of her leave and then a further 12 weeks at the statutory limit. A small employer can claim back 100% of the amount paid to the woman, plus compensation of 4.5%. A larger employer can claim back only 92% of the amount. To qualify as a small employer the firm's gross National Insurance bill (both employees' and employer's contributions) must have been less than a specified sum in the previous tax year.

All the evidence shows that children tend to become better people if they are looked after by a parent, normally the mother, in the early years. The government however makes a payment not to the woman who stays at home to look after the child but to the woman who goes back to work. This payment sends the wrong message.

It is unreasonable that an employer should have to take any responsibility for paying maternity benefit and then have to reclaim all or some of it. If the state feels that payment is due, it should make it direct.

In November 2014 the DWP provided advice on the implementation of the Maternity Allowance (Curtailment) Regulations which allows a woman to complete her maternity Allowance early so that an eligible person (spouse, civil partner or the child's father) can take the remaining number of untaken weeks leave of Maternity Allowance as shared parental pay.

(c) Help for lone parents

Lone parent benefit

One particular form of income support causes special concern: payments to lone parents.

In the first place there should be no such things as a lone parent payment.

Each child is born as a result of intercourse between a man and a woman and they are jointly responsible for bringing up their child. That people must always be responsible for the consequences of their actions is a prime maxim of the good society. It is no good protesting that the father does not and can not pay for the care of his child. He must pay and the state must ensure that he has the means to pay. How this can be done is explained in Part II of this book. If there is any doubt as to the paternity DNA can be checked. In any case the name of the father and mother must be registered when the baby is born.

It is the state's job to help people become their best selves and that means helping parents to care for a child mainly from their own resources or with the help of their own parents but also with the assistance of money from the state available to every child's parents on the basis of fairness.

What governments in the UK have chosen to do is to give income support and other financial benefits to unmarried parents (normally mothers) of children under 16 which are not available to married or self-sufficient parents, taking money in taxes from the responsible and giving it in benefit to those who have been irresponsible. In addition, preference has been given to single parents in the allocation of council accommodation. The state has in fact taken on the role formerly expected of a father.

Not surprisingly young girls without strong academic ambition take advantage of the state's generosity.

In the late 1970's one baby in ten was born to an unmarried mother, in 1986 two in ten and in 1997 nearly four in ten (37%). Among women under twenty, the rate was almost nine in ten.

In 1995, one quarter of births were not registered by both parents while less than three quarters of those who did register shared parents of the same address.

A study by the O.N.S. (Office for National Statistics) seen and reported on by the Sunday Times (17/10/04) revealed that one in four single mothers may have opted out of a traditional family environment for financial reasons. It says the women have a 'regular partner who lives elsewhere' and there are 'financial disincentives' that encourage couples to live apart.

A controversial study was carried out by John Haskey, a leading expert on the family. Haskey found that 1.2 million couples in long-term relationships choose to live apart – but the rate among single mothers is almost twice the national average.

In 2004, more than 830,000 lone parents lived on welfare benefits, claiming income support, child allowances and housing benefit, costing a total of £14 billion a year.

Previous studies have shown that lone parents who marry stand to lose between 7% and 28% of their income. Haskey's research suggests more than 200,000 may be choosing to live apart to maximise their benefits. Others may be defrauding the system by failing to declare cohabiting partners.

Likewise the system of tax-credits which Gordon Brown introduced as Chancellor has favoured single parents at the expense of married couples. In the words of Frank Field, writing in the Sunday Times (08/07/07) "just look at how Brown's tax credit system wallops two-parent families. A single parent with two children working 16 hours a week will gain a weekly income after tax credit payments of £487. The breadwinner of a two-parent family, also with two children, will be required to work 116 hours to get the same income. Such effort is impossible to sustain for more than a week or two".

Robert Rowthorn, Professor of Economics at Cambridge said "the system of benefits offers a very strong incentive for people to remain as lone parents. I am sure Gordon Brown's system of tax credits has made it worse"

Under-age sex and consequent pregnancies also greatly increased. Official figures reported in the Times (23/02/07) showed that 7,917 girls aged 15 and under became pregnant in 2005, up 4% on the year before, an under-age conception rate of 7.8 per thousand girls. The government has given teenagers greater access to condoms, the morning-after pill and sex education. Teenage pregnancies including all girls aged 18 and under totalled 42,187 in that year. In the second decade of the twenty first century however teenage pregnancies reduced.

What the state should do is to ensure that both parents, mother and father, take full responsibility for meeting the cost of bringing up the children and to give the same support to all parents. How this can be done will be explained in Part II of this book.

The close presence of the mother – and father to some extent – is a vital factor influencing the development of the child in the early years. For a mother to choose to go to work and leave the child in the care of a nanny can be harmful to the child. But it is the child's future as a citizen that matters most.

Yet the state is harrying mothers because they are not attending job interviews.

In January 2014 the government made clear that if lone parents received income support they must actively look for work. Advisers would arrange work-focused interviews for lone parents, aged 18 and over, with a youngest child aged one to four, who is entitled to income support solely on the basis of being a lone parent or if they are entitled to employment and support allowance (ESA).

DWP statistics published in November 2014 showed that between April 2004 and June 2014 inclusive, 10,071,900 work focused interviews were attended by income support lone parent claimants while in the year up to and including June 2014, 580,000 such interviews were conducted.

The state moreover punishes lone parents for not attending these interviews. In the year up to and including June 2014, there were 42,300 sanctions imposed on income support lone parent claimants. Some claims moreover were sanctioned more than once, such that 39,100 individual income support lone parent claims incurred a sanction in that 12 month period.

(d) Child Support Allowance (Child Maintenance Service)

Where parents have separated the government expects non resident parents to make regular payments to the caring parents. It has, where necessary, paid Child Support Allowance (CSA) to the caring parent.

In the summer of 2014 the DWP began to transfer Child Support Agency (CSA) clients to the Child Maintenance Service.

The changes were due to take place between 2014 and 2017 and from July 2014 the CSA began writing to clients to let them know that the child maintenance arrangements they currently had would be ending.

In addition, the CSA would give parents six months notice of when their individual arrangements would change. When their CSA arrangements ended, parents would be able to either make a family-based arrangement where they agree between themselves what to pay and when or to make an application to the Child Maintenance Service if they cannot come to an agreement themselves.

(e) Child Care Allowance

The future of our country depends upon the quality of its citizens. Their quality will depend on the way they are brought up as children. Research has shown that close attachment to a loving parent in the early years is a vital factor in the development of their intellectual and moral quality.

Government has given parents Child Benefit as mentioned in section 6 (a) above. A responsible government might be expected to give an additional allowance to parents where either father or mother was at home with their child during the early years of 1 to 5.

Incredibly, the government in recent times has given Childcare Allowance not to those parents who look after their child but to those who wish to work and to leave their children at day centres providing care.

In March 2013 the government announced a plan to offer childcare vouchers of up to £1,200 p.a. per child. It expected to phase in the new plan from the autumn of 2015, starting with children under 5 in the first year and then extending it to those under 12. The new scheme would apply only to families where both parents were in work and would not cover those on Tax Credits or on the new Universal Credit which was soon to come into effect.

Under the scheme households would be able to apply for childcare vouchers online and would receive a proportion of their yearly childcare costs of up to £6,000 per child. Where childcare costs were lower, the vouchers would be worth proportionally less. Parents would be able to use the vouchers for any Ofsted-regulated childcare.

In March 2014 however, the Prime Minister announced that a more generous package would come more quickly than planned. Families earning up to £150,000 a year would be eligible for tax-breaks to help with the costs of nurseries, nannies and other care for children up to the age of 12.

Instead of being introduced gradually over seven years the government set an ambitious timetable for the new childcare voucher scheme to be fully operational in only 12 months – by the autumn of 2015.

The scheme, to be run by National Savings and Investments enables working parents to deposit part of their income into childcare accounts online. For every 80p paid in, the Government adds 20p up to a maximum of £2,000 per child. Only registered childcare providers would be able to be paid from this fund.

The government made the scheme more accessible to part-time workers and those running their own business. Parents would have to earn a minimum of £50 a week and work for at least 8 hours to qualify.

To be eligible, both partners in two-parent households must work and earn between £2,600 and £150,000. Single parents qualify if they meet the income requirements, as will carers and those on maternity or paternity leave.

However, the tax break would not be available to couples in which only one parent earns, despite calls for more help for parents who choose not to work. The scheme was expected to help about 1.9 million working parents of children aged 12 or under, at a cost of about £750 million.

By February 2015 (as reported by the Independent 15/2/15) more than half of councils were 'failing' to provide appropriate child care. Barely two-in-five local authorities in England provided enough nursery places, holiday and breakfast clubs or after-school services for parents who work full-time, down from 54 per cent the previous year.

In the middle of the twentieth century, Britain was far poorer than it is in the early twenty first century. Yet parents were then able to look after their children properly at home. It was not necessary – as well as not desirable –

that both parents should work. What a mess we have made of our country that children now have to be taken from their home to be looked after in day-care centres.

On the 1st June 2015, the Prime Minister made clear that from September 2016 the government will pay for 30 free hours of childcare per week for children aged three and four. Only those households where both parents are working or single-parent households where the adult is in work will be eligible for more than the present allowance of 15 hours.

Mr Cameron has made clear that the enhanced childcare is conditional on every adult in a household working. More than a million families are already benefiting from 15 hours a week of free childcare for three and four year olds, as well as around 160,000 of the most disadvantaged two year olds. The government has also legislated to introduce tax free childcare worth up to £2,000 a year.

The Resolution Foundation, adding to the pressure published in early 2015 a report praising measures "which would help to lift children out of poverty by helping some mothers into jobs and boosting family income" (Times 8/6/15).

As reported by Rosemary Bennett in the Times (24/6/15) the EU has lamented the fact that so many mothers stay at home to look after their children. British women were twice as likely to give up work to look after children or elderly relatives as their EU counterparts, largely because of the lack of subsidised childcare. When they did return to work, the jobs were likely to be part time and poorly paid. Unaffordable childcare is the most common problem cited by mothers for not returning to work after giving birth.

Laura Perrins of the campaign group Mothers at home Matter, said the pressure to work showed no regard to children. "How British families organise their care is up to them" she said. "They shouldn't be lectured to by the government or bean counters in Europe."

What Laura Perrins said was right. How well we bring up our own children is what matters.

What really matters is living a good life and helping others to live a good life. Since the late twentieth century what matters is seen as having things and having enough money to own more things.

In the summer of 2015 Steve Hilton's book was published under the title 'More Human: Designing a World Where People Come First'. He shows how what matters to children's development is the family in which they are brought up. Their brains need to be stimulated by frequent communication with their parents. They develop best if they are cared for by a mother and father who are married or at least utterly committed to each other. 'At the age of 3', reports Hilton, 'rich kids, in settled families, have heard about 30m more words than poor children not living in an effective family'. The brains of such children do not develop nearly as well as those in a positive family background.

As Tim Montgomerie reported in the Times (8/6/15) Labour leader contender Liz Kendal wants to address why some deprived children start school as much as 20 months behind their peers on some key measures of development – and never catch up.

Steve Hilton, as has been shown, is also an advocate of early intervention.

Recognising that a child's key brain functions develop in their first few years he wants a massive increase in health visitors to help new parents acquire basic child-rearing skills. He also wants parenting classes, provided by voluntary organisations, to become the social norm.

This government agrees in theory and helped the Labour MP Graham Allen to establish the Early Intervention Foundation. The EIF has estimated that the failure of many parents to give their youngsters a healthy diet, read with them regularly or set clear boundaries is resulting in social problems from obesity to criminality that cost taxpayers £17 billion every year. For Allen, preventing children from doing wrong in the first place could be "the biggest deficit-reduction programme imaginable" and he has identified 19 programmes that are proven to make a difference. Unfortunately there are few votes in stopping problems that are still a decade or more downstream.

The failure of the government and of some parents to put children first over the early years of the twenty first century has led to predictable results. Emily Duggan, social affairs editor of the Sunday Times reported (18/6/15) that record numbers of children were referred to social services in England in 2014, as 570,800 minors were identified as at risk in England in a single year. In Scotland, 4,606 were added to the child protection register in 2014; an increase of 133 per cent since 2002.

Social services are working with 80 per cent more children than they were in 2002, according to official figures. The NSPCC's helpline also saw a significant rise in adults contacting them about a child's welfare, with 61,709 getting in touch in 2014, up from 21 per cent from 2012/13.

The prime purpose of society must be to ensure that children are brought up in the best possible way so that they become first-class citizens in the future. Clearly the government should be giving support to the parents who provide the best possible care with one of them always at home with a young child. Instead it helps pay for children to be looked after elsewhere. How this can be changed is explained in Part II

However working parents have one very strong argument to explain what they do.

Why do both parents work?

Working mothers often argue that they work primarily for economic reasons. Carol Midgley, in the Times (04/10/05) commented: "It is blindingly obvious that a mother is, ideally, the best person to look after her child. We don't need a seven-year survey to tell us that. But what are we supposed to do about it? Suddenly conjure up a winning lottery ticket? The vast majority of mothers go to work because they have to. This, after all, is the real world, where mortgages and bills must be paid".

ONS figures relating to 2005 showed that 71% of mothers would stay at home with the children if money was no object. In fact 56% of women of working age with children under 5 were in employment. Roger Semmens, in a letter to the Sunday Times (25/01/07) made a similar point: "High house prices mean both partners have to work (and for more hours than in other countries) to pay for the mortgage. This results in less quality in the way children are brought up. Unless both parents work, they find it very difficult to afford the cost of a mortgage, given current house prices. The only way to meet the mortgage cost is often that both continue to work apart from a few months when the baby is born. The baby has to be looked after by others and the children are far more likely to grow up unhappy and badly behaved than would have been the case had they had a parent to care for them."

So the huge increase in housing prices which government failed to check is one important factor helping to lead to the breakdown of society.

Measures must be taken to reduce the cost of renting or buying a home. How this might be done is explained in Part II.

7. *Tax Credits*

Speenhamland

In 1795 the village of Speenhamland decided to make payments to those who were not earning enough to be able to pay themselves for what they needed. The Speenhamland System spread across the country.

There are however defects in such a system. The employer may feel that he does not need to pay a proper wage because the employee will be provided from public funds for the extra he needs. This may also discourage employers from attempting more efficient labour-saving ways of working. The system was abandoned in the 1830's.

Gordon Brown as Chancellor of the Exchequer in the Labour government, decided to re-instate the Speenhamland system through a system of tax credits which were fully implemented in April 2003. The government sought to identify precisely what needs people had and then to ensure they had financial support to enable them to satisfy these needs.

(a) *Child Tax Credit*

The Child Tax Credit provided money to all families with an income of less than a specified sum. In order to qualify, they had to have at least one child under the age of 16 (until the 1st September following their birthday), or under 19 if in full-time education or under 18 if not working more than 24 hours pw. (or with incomes of less than a specific sum if there was a child under 1 year old). Families with incomes of up to a specific sum received some payment. Neither parent was required to be in work.

The size of the award depended on the number of children and income levels of the family. One and two-earner couples were treated equally, so a single-earner family with an income of £40,000 would receive the same credit as a couple where both partners earned £20,000.

The maximum credit – then £5,625 for parents with 3 children – would be paid until earnings reached a specific sum. Thereafter it was withdrawn at a rate of 37p for every pound until the credit reached £545. It remained at that level for incomes up to £50,000 when it again tapered off. In the first year of a child's life, parents receiving Child Tax Benefit were given an extra £545 a year. Although called a "credit", the award was deposited directly into the bank account of the carer, usually the mother.

By 2012 parents could get some child credit so long as their income was not over the limit of £41,300. It was a complex system requiring a great deal of checking by the government employees responsible.

To qualify for the childcare element, parents, if part of a couple, must work at least 16 hours a week. The credit was originally worth up to 70p in every pound (raised to 80p for 2007/08) spent on approved childcare, up to a limit (in 2007/08) of £175 a week for one child and £300 a week for two or more children. So if someone spent £80 a week on childcare and was on a very low income, they would receive £56. The amount decreased as income levels rose. Payments were made directly to the parent responsible for caring for the child.

(b) Working Tax Credit

The Working Tax Credit has been a top-up payment for people on low incomes. It has aimed to entice people into employment, whether they have children or not. After it was introduced, the system was seen to be complete. Couples with joint incomes of up to a specified sum and single people earning a lesser sum benefit. People with children or a disability need to work 16 hours a week while others must be aged over 25 and work 30 hours. These criteria were relaxed for people over 50 returning to work after receiving out-of-work benefits and for the disabled.

Income or joint income and number of hours worked determined the size of the award. The maximum award was for people who worked more than

30 hours but who earned less than a specified sum. A minimum sum was paid to parents who worked between 16 and 30 hours per week. After the maximum award was reached, the credit was reduced.

If employed, the employer has to add the credit to pay. The self-employed have it paid directly into their bank accounts. If both partners in a couple have worked more than 16 hours a week, they were able to elect which one received the credit.

Claiming Tax Credits

Those wanting to benefit have had to fill in a claim form and return it to the Inland Revenue by April 6th in any year. The claimants provide income details for the previous tax year. Once set, the award ran for the full tax year but could be adjusted if one's income falls in the current year. The credit would also be adjusted if one's income rose by more than a specified sum. At the end of the tax year the award would be reconciled against actual income for the previous year and an over-payment or an under-payment calculated.

(c) Tax Credit Problems

The government spent £9m on a national television advertising campaign to promote the new tax credit (Times 08/03/03). Nevertheless take-up was a long way short of the target and many problems emerged from this vast, complex operation. Where 6m families claimed credits, each of which had to be worked out, mistakes were almost bound to happen.

In December 2003, for instance, some low income families suddenly found they were receiving lower credits as the Inland Revenue sought to recover earlier overpayments. According to The Times (23/12/03) the National Association of Citizen's Advice Bureaux (NACAB) said that it had been inundated with requests for assistance. It identified two types of families affected by the claw backs of the Child Tax and Working Tax Credits: those whose financial circumstances changed during the course of the year and those who had fallen victim to Inland Revenue error.

Because the new tax credits were based on income information from the 2001/02 financial year, the Inland Revenue adjusted payouts to claimants if their circumstances altered. This adjustment normally took the form of a 'claw back', a reduction in benefit payments designed to cancel out the earlier overpayment.

A NACAB spokesman said: "The Inland Revenue gave people money based on an estimate of their case and they are now saying that they want their extra money back. People are not being advised that this is happening. They just see that their payment has dropped".

The second class of families seeing their benefits cut were those who received over-payments earlier in the year because of Inland Revenue error, the NACAB said.

The Treasury said that in the overwhelming majority of cases tax credit payments had been reduced because the claimants' personal circumstances had changed. Only a handful had been overpaid because of Inland Revenue error. A spokesman added that the Inland Revenue would not be clawing back overpayments resulting from its own errors if claimants could not have reasonably been expected to know that their payments were wrong.

Another problem caused by overpayments is illustrated by the case of David Nicholds, reported by Alex Hawkes (Times 23/12/03).

Mr Nicholds was told that his child tax credits had been based on an estimate of his salary from the previous year. He was then paid a bonus at work, thus increasing his salary and decreasing his eligibility for the tax credit. That meant that he should not have received £900 over the course of the 2002-03 tax year which he then had to pay back.

Mr Nicholds was initially told that the £900 would be due by January 31st 2004 as a lump sum but was then told that he would be able to pay instalments of £70 a month starting in April.

The Times (15/04/06) gave another example of the costing in human terms in this complex benefit. When Gordon Brown introduced Tax Credits in 2003 Serena Furniss and her husband Nikolas regarded the scheme as a lifeline to help them look after their six children (Helen Nugent wrote). Three years later the tax man had clawed back nearly £7,000 of overpayments, leaving the family with what they said would amount to a lifetime of debt. When the revenue told Mrs Furniss that it would be cutting her child tax credit by 70% to make up for the months of overpayment she was left with no option but to re-mortgage their house. But that was not enough.

For a year the family lived on credit cards and struggled to meet their basic bills, such as their weekly shopping trip. "Now we will be paying for the Revenue's mistakes for the next 20 years", Mrs Furniss from the Isle-of-Wight, said.

A report on tax credits from the cross-party Public Accounts Committee, published in April 2006, said that Revenue & Customs attempted to recover an estimated £2.2 billion from vulnerable families for the second consecutive year in 2004-05, despite a public outcry over its actions. The Revenue paid out £15.8 billion in tax credits to about 6 million families in 2004-05. After assessing payouts for the previous year, it disclosed a total overpayment of £2.2 billion to 1.9 million families. "The department estimates that there will be a similar level of overpayments for 2004-05 awards", the Public Accounts Committee's report said.

A Citizen's Advice survey in October 2007 (Times 16/10/07) revealed that a quarter of respondents would definitely not want to claim again and a further one in four were less likely to claim in the future. For too many people, the uncertainty, anxiety and hardship claiming tax credits can cause outweighs the benefits of the extra money they provide according to David Harker, chief executive of Citizen's Advice.

Such problems had a devastating impact on family life, especially when claimants were suddenly forced to re-pay overpayments. Some respondents re-mortgaged, becoming ill and stressed, or relied on others for basic provisions. In 2006/07, the charity dealt with a 21% rise in tax credit problems and survey respondents weren't slow to apportion blame. One said, "The whole system is a shambles and the government should hang its head in shame at what they have done to some of the neediest families in Britain."

Gordon Brown introduced tax credits because he thought they would help poorer people. But good intentions are not enough; those in government must have the wisdom to understand how society works.

It is fair to say that the Treasury did overcome some of the problems and improve the service. According to national statistics for 2006/07 published by HM Revenue & Customs (HMRC) in May 2008 overpayments of tax credits had fallen by £700 million from 2005/06 to 2006/07 and were less than half the level they had been in 2003/04. The figures showed that in 2006/07 the total of overpayment was £1 billion compared with £2.2 billion in 2003/04. The Treasury also pointed out that 5.96 million families were benefiting from tax credits.

Nevertheless it is still the case that millions of people are assessed by civil servants who decide on the basis of complex rules how much their total income should be and on that basis how much the state should give them – and then still very often get it wrong.

It really makes no sense to operate such a complex and confusing system. But in the years from 2007 to 2013 the government and the civil servants operating the scheme must surely have made the system simpler and fairer.

(d) 2014 Guide

In 2014 the HMRC published a guide for people wishing to claim tax credits. It reads as follows:-

How to work out usual working hours for your tax credits claim

You need to work a minimum number of hours each week to get Working Tax Credit. The way you calculate your working hours depends on what sort of work you do.

How many hours do you have to work each week?

The hours you need to work to get Working Tax Credit depends on your circumstances, including whether or not you have children. You should expect your paid work to continue for at least four weeks.

If you don't have children

To get Working Tax Credit you must normally be aged 25 or over and work at least 30 hours or more a week. But you only need to work 16 hours or more a week if you:

- have a disability and are aged at least 16

- are aged 60 or over

If you have children

To get Working Tax Credit you need to be aged at least 16 and working the following hours:

If you're single, you need to work at least 16 hours a week

If you're in a couple your joint working hours need to be at least 24 a week, with one of you working at least 16 hours a week.

So if you're in a couple and only one of you is working, that person must be working at least 24 hours a week.

If your joint working hours are less than 24 a week, you can still get working tax credit if one of the following applies:

- one of you is aged 60 or over and working at least 16 hours a week

- one of you is disabled and working at least 16 hours a week

- one of you works at least 16 hours a week and the other person is entitled to Carer's Allowance – even if they don't get any payments because they receive other benefits instead

- one of you works at least 16 hours a week and the other person is 'incapacitated', an in-patient in hospital, or in prison (serving a custodial sentence, or remanded in custody awaiting trial or sentence).

How to work out your usual weekly working hours

You'll need to put the number of hours you usually work in a week on your tax credits claim form. You only count hours for which you are paid – don't include unpaid lunch hours.

If you're an employee

Give the total number of hours you usually work and are paid for in a week for all jobs that you do. If you normally work overtime, include this. If your hours vary from week to week, put down what you and your employer(s) think of as your normal number of paid hours.

If you're self-employed

Put down the number of hours you normally spend working in your business, either on work billed to the client or related activity, for example:

- trips to wholesalers and retailers

- visits to potential clients

- time spent on advertising

- cleaning the business premises

- cleaning a vehicle used as part of the business, for example a taxi

- book-keeping

- research work

If you work from home, include time spent travelling to see customers.

If you have only just become self-employed, use the number or hours you normally expect to work in a week.

If you're a seasonal worker

If you do seasonal work, or your hours change over the year, show the hours you're working at the time you make your claim.

If you do regular term-time work

If you work a regular number of hours a week, but only during the school term, put down the hours you work during term-time.

If you do agency work

You work pattern may change from week to week, depending on how much work the agency has for you. You and your employer must decide how many hours you usually work. Just being registered with an agency and being available for work isn't enough to qualify.

If you do on-call work

If you do on-call work, your working hours are those which you are called out. For example, you are called out four nights in a week for four hours at a time. Your total hours for that week would be 16 (4 nights x 4 hours = 16 hours in total).

If you're on standby

If you're on standby and have no fixed pattern of work, tell the Tax Credit Office what you expect your normal hours to be. Don't count time on standby, when you are not paid. For example, you expect to be called out three nights a week for seven hours at a time. Your normal anticipated hours would be 21 per week (3 nights x 7 hours per night = 21 hours per week in total).

Changes in your working hours

Your hours drop – or you stop work

You must tell the Tax Credit Office within one month if your hours of work fall below the minimum for your circumstances. To find out the minimum working hours, see 'How many hours do you have to work each week?'

You also need to get in touch within one month if any of the following happen:

- you or your partner were working at least 30 hours a week and your hours have dropped to less than 30 hours a week

- you're in a couple with children and your joint working hours drop to less than 30 a week.

- you or your partner stop working

If you don't report these changes you may get paid too much money, which you may have to pay back. You may also have to pay a penalty.

Your hours go up

You should tell the Tax Credit Office as soon as possible if:

- Your usual hours of paid work go up

- Your income goes up because you're now working more hours

You may be able to get more tax credits if your hours go up. Any extra payments can only usually be backdated for up to one month.

If your increased hours also mean an increase in income, then your tax credit payments could go down. This is because the amount of tax credits you get depends on the amount of money you have coming in. Tell the Tax Credit Office about your increased income. If you don't, you may be getting too much in tax credits – an overpayment – which you will have to pay back.

The arrangements for the payment of the credits have not been simplified. If anything they have become more complex. The army of civil servants we employ to check and operate the scheme costs even more millions of pounds than before. The British government and parliament should be ashamed of approving such as crazy system.

But if you are receiving disability benefits for yourself, your child or your partner there are even more complex rules to study. In 2014, HMRC set these out as follows:

If you're claiming disability benefits for yourself or your child you may qualify for extra tax credits – on top of other benefits you're getting. Some disability benefits are also taken into account when the Tax Credit Office works out how much tax credits you're entitled to.

What are the benefits that can help you qualify for extra tax credits?

If you or your partner are working and have a disability

Certain sickness or disability related benefits that you might get – or have recently been getting – can help you qualify for extra Working Tax Credit. For example:

- you could be getting a benefit such as Disability Living Allowance or Personal Independence Payment

- you might recently have been getting a benefit like Incapacity Benefit or Employment Support Allowance

If you or your partner have a severe disability

You or your partner might get one of the following:

- Highest rate Care component of Disability Living Allowance

- Higher rate of Attendance Allowance

- Enhanced Daily Living component of Personal Independence Payment

If so, you may qualify for a further amount of Working Tax Credit because of your severe disability. In a couple, the person with the severe disability doesn't have to be working - as long as one of you is.

If your child has a disability

You can get extra Child Tax Credit if one of the following benefits is paid for your child:

- Disability Living Allowance

- Personal Independence Payment

This still applies even if the allowance or payment has stopped because your child is in hospital. You can also get extra Child Tax Credit if your child is registered blind.

You have a child with a disability – Can you get extra Child Tax Credit?

How much extra tax credits can you get?

In this tax year (6th April 2014 – 5th April 2015), on top of your basic tax credits you could get:

- Up to £2,935 a year, that is around £56 a week, if you are disabled

- Up to £4,190 a year, that is around £81 a week, if you are severely disabled

- £3,100 a year, that is around £60 a week, if your child is disabled

- £4,355 a year, that is around £84 a week, if your child is severely disabled

The amount of credits you are paid depends on other income you have coming in. The higher your income, the lower your tax credit payments.

(e) Fraud & Error in Tax Credits

Having such a complex system leads to error and waste and vulnerability to fraud.

In June 2014 HMRC published tax credits and error statistics for 2012-2013. Estimates based on random samples of cases concluded that over £2bn was overpaid whilst £200m was underpaid.

The statistics set out estimates based on analysis of a random sample of child tax credit and working tax credit cases and concluded that error favouring the claimant accounted for 3.1 per cent of finalised entitlement, amounting to £800m while fraud favouring the claimant to £1.13bn.

Error favouring HMRC accounted for 0.7 per cent of finalised entitlement, amounting to £200m.

In 2014, for the third successive year the National Audit Office (NAO) qualified its audit on the HMRC 2013/14 accounts due to error and fraud in tax credits.

In its report on the HMRC 2013/2014 accounts, the NAO found significant levels of error and fraud within the tax credits system equating to payments of between £1.8 bn and £2.2 bn being made to claimants because of error or fraud and a further £70 mn to £320 mn not being paid to claimants because of error.

Of six identified risk areas the report found that there had been an increase in error and fraud in areas relating to undeclared partners, work and hours and disability. However, there had been a decrease in error and fraud in the remaining three risk areas relating to income, children and childcare costs. In conclusion the report recommended that 'HMRC should investigate why the levels or error and fraud in personal tax credits associated with undeclared partners have continued to rise despite its initiatives undertaken to date to tackle this specific risk.'

Annual Review

Each year the rates of payment and sometimes the condition have to be reviewed. In April 2014 for instance, the Tax Credits Up-rating Regulations (SI.No.845/2014):

- increased the maximum rates of the disabled and severely disabled elements of child tax credit for a child and qualifying young person;

- increased the maximum rates of the disability element and severe disability element of working tax credit; and

- increased the first income threshold for those entitled to child tax credit only, to £16,010.

At the same time new regulations were issued in relation to late tax credit appeals. The Credits (Late Appeals) Order (SI.No.885/2014) restored the ability of HMRC to accept late tax credit appeals, in exceptional circumstances, for up the 12 months following the normal 30-day time limit.

(f) Criticism of Tax Credit

Tax credits have cost the taxpayer more than £30 bn pa and a great deal of this has to be spent on administration because of the extreme complexity of the rules which have determined the level of tax credit given to different people in different situations. Many government employees must be engaged in finding out how much should be given to a particular claimant. Frankly the system is mad. The fact that employees can apply for working tax credit enables firms to pay them less. This was demonstrated by Janice Turner in the Times (4/10/14). A survey of Sainsbury's employees by Unite in 2013 found that 60% relied upon government working tax credits to top up their salaries.

It may be argued that if the system is so crazy why has it not been altered. But if large numbers of citizens have been relying on their tax credits it will not be easy to take them away. However Frank Field, veteran Labour MP was elected as Chairman of the Work and Pensions Committee after the 2015 General Election and he thinks the job can be done over 5 years of a parliament if linked to a rise in the minimum wage.

In comments reported by Sam Coates in the Times (3/7/15) Mr Field said new claimants should be barred from claiming tax credits immediately, while top-ups for those already claiming should be continued until 2020, before being phased out. "Successive Chancellors have been responsible for making businesses welfare dependent by offering to top up people on particularly low wages", he said. "We should realise as politicians that we have responsibility for creating a new army of dependency: employers. Instead of saying I'm going to make the savings (on tax credits) this year, I would make them by the end of the parliament. So they are phased in. But you can start by making the savings immediately for new claimants." He added: "We should have a very soft landing for existing claimants whose employers will in no way be able to match losses in tax credits with increases in wages – though that should be the aim by the end of the parliament. Welfare dependency among employers is one of the many reasons we have low productivity in this country."

To compensate for the loss of this subsidy, Mr Field said that the Low Pay Commission, which sets the minimum wage, should be replaced with a "fair wages commission". It would push as many sectors as possible to pay the living wage.

David Cameron, in his speech at Runcorn on 22nd June 2015 seemed to support the plan to cut tax credits and raise the minimum wage when he said that "we need to move from a low wage, high tax, high welfare society to a higher wage, lower tax, lower welfare society."

George Osborne, Chancellor of the Exchequer, made some moves toward the reduction of tax credits in his budget of 2015. His move to limit child tax credits to the first two children in a family would apply to all children born from April 2017. The cut would save the government £315 million in the first year. Later in 2015 however the Chancellor had to drop this proposal.

8. Special help for older citizens

Winter fuel allowance

The state makes a number of payments to older citizens. They receive a winter fuel allowance: in 2013/14 this was £200 pw for those over 70 and £300 for those over 80. This cost the government £2 bn in 2015/16 according to Treasury figures published in the Times (9/7/15).

Mr Cameron in a televised debate before the 2010 election, promised not to touch their benefits. The Conservative Party relies on the votes of older people to secure elections and Mr Cameron did not want to alienate them.

But should the state be paying out some 3 billion pounds a year to all its older citizens?

Some older citizens, for instance, have retired to spend their time in Spain or other countries which are mild in winter and they are also entitled to receive the winter fuel allowance. In September 2014 government figures found by the Taxpayer's Alliance showed that in 2013/14 £55.9m was paid to 49,970 pensioners in Spain while £29.8m was paid to 29,535 pensioners in France and £8.5m to 8,170 pensioners in Cyprus.

Some argue that such pensioners should not receive the allowance but what about those who go to Spain and then return to Britain? Deciding where to draw the line would lead to a new administrative system to sort out cases as fairly as possible.

There have been moves not to give these benefits to the wealthier pensioners.

Mr Duncan-Smith in April 2013 said that those who did not need the money should return it to the treasury. "It's up to them, if they don't want it, to hand it back" he said (Times 29/4/13). But this means that those who act to help others lose their money but those who are too greedy or too busy to do this still keep it for their own purposes.

In September 2014 the King's Fund recommended that the winter fuel allowances should be means-tested.

The problem with this is how to set the point at which they cease to get these benefits. In any case, this involves means-testing which is always unfair and administratively more expensive.

If an older person with an income of £20,000 pa does not receive the benefit while someone earning £19,500 pa does receive it this creates unfairness as well as more administrative costs.

In February 2015 Policy Exchange argued (Times 3/2/15) that pensioners should opt in to winter fuel payments rather than get them automatically, saving up to £400 million a year. Policy Exchange argued that it was a waste of money to give this to wealthy pensioners who do not need extra cash to help with fuel bills.

However, instead of means-testing the benefit (which would cost £2 billion a year) they suggest pensioners should tick a box if they want to receive the amount of £200 or £300 a year.

Would it not be better to scrap the benefit and create a society in which all older citizens have sufficient income to pay for fuel?

Free TV licence

People over 75 are also entitled to receive a free TV licence. In September 2014 the King's Fund recommended that this, like the winter fuel allowance, should be means-tested. But means-testing creates unfairness while someone over 75 is not necessarily in greater need of financial help. Moreover the process increases government hassle and costs. In 2015 the Chancellor of the Exchequer passed to the BBC responsibility for paying for these licences. Surely it would be better to ensure that we have a society in which people of any age are able to afford a TV licence?

Bus passes

Older people are also able to have free bus passes.

This work is arguing that benefits are either unjust or wasteful or both and that we should have a society in which people are able to look after their own affairs. But if there is to be one exception it must be this. People who are well off and have a car will not claim a free bus pass. Older people without a car may be able to have a fuller life by having one.

National insurance exemption

In September 2014 the King's Fund also questioned the practice of allowing those over 65 to continue to work but to be excused from making national insurance payments. This however is not a benefit but one of many indefensible parts of the national insurance system.

9. Incapacity Benefit (Employment Support Allowance)

Inability to work as a result of injury or illness may remove the capacity of some people to earn their own living and the state has long accepted responsibility for providing an income in these circumstances. The number receiving this benefit has been extraordinarily high: 2.7 million people in January 2005 and still 2.64 million in 2007.

There have been many stories of people both working and drawing incapacity benefit at the same time. People receiving this benefit have been very reluctant to give it up since if they fail to make a go of it at work it may not be easy to get the benefit restored. The fact that the amount of benefit increased after a year encouraged some to stay incapacitated long enough to qualify for the higher sum. Doctors have been inclined to certify a patient's incapacity as the most helpful thing they can do at no cost to themselves.

The Labour government legislated to reduce the number on incapacity benefit by separating claimants who wanted to work from those who were unable to do so. The reforms that came into effect in October 2008 removed the 'perverse incentive' for claimants to stay on IB, as the amount rose after a year. Under the new system, claimants were entitled to a 'holding benefit' paid at the same level as Jobseeker's Allowance – until they were assessed by a doctor within 12 weeks of making their claim. Those assessed as being unable to work would receive a disability and sickness allowance, worth more than the previous incapacity rate.

The rest would go to a rehabilitation support allowance worth much less. This would be supplemented by a further sum each week if they agreed to attend work-focused interviews, training and rehabilitation.

There was a mixed response to these arrangements when they were proposed in 2005. Disability organisations cautioned that junior Jobcentre Plus staff might pressure people attending work-focused interviews to look for work when they were too ill to do so.

Cliff Prior, the Chief Executive of the mental health charity Rethink, said the proposals could force people with fluctuating mental health conditions either to argue that they were too ill to ever work again in order to get the higher benefit or to take the risk of accepting lower benefit in order to get employment support in the knowledge that their condition could worsen in the future. But the government had to take action to deal with the basic problem: the fact, justified by many examples, that many on incapacity benefit could in fact work.

Nevertheless, many people on incapacity benefit do have real mental health problems. According to figures released in February 2007 (Times 01/02/07) more than 100,000 people received the benefit because they suffered from anxiety, a third higher than in 1997. There had also been a large increase in the numbers who claimed it on the grounds of stress.

What was particularly worrying was the number of young people on incapacity benefit. Figures from the Department for Work and Pensions (DWP) released in 2008 (Times 04/01/08) showed that in May 2007 120,000 adults aged 18 to 34 had been on incapacity benefit or severe disablement allowance for five years or more. A further 130,000 had been on the benefit for at least two years.

In total 504,000 people under 35 were claiming incapacity benefit in 2007 compared with 443,000 claiming Jobseeker's Allowance, the data showed.

A spokesman for the DWP said that 300,000 of the 504,000 young people claiming sickness benefit in May 2007 had mental and behavioural disorders.

Sue Christoforou of Mind, the mental health charity, said that society was faster paced, the workplace more competitive and there were more short-term contracts, which all placed extra stress on workers. Paul Bivand, a welfare-to-work expert at Inclusion, a think-tank, said: "There is a second generation of people coming on to incapacity benefits for mental reasons. This may well be due to ingrained hopelessness."

It has been argued that the existence of incapacity benefit has done real harm to the lives of young people. Karen Graham, head of incapacity benefit at Reed in Partnership, a welfare-to-work company used by the government, emphasised the difficulty many young jobless people faced, especially those caught up in a generational cycle of worklessness. "These are families that have never worked and there is a culture of not working that has a significant impact on young people," she said.

By 2010, as reported in the Sunday Times (2/5/10), there were 2 million people receiving incapacity benefit at a cost to the country of £12 billion a year.

Mr Duncan-Smith, Secretary of State for Work and Pensions in the coalition government formed in May 2010 was determined to reduce the cost of incapacity benefit, then £12 billion p.a. and to get people back to work as soon as possible. To signify this approach the benefit was to be re-named the Employment Support Allowance (ESA). He allocated £5 billion to a work programme which paid charities and other organisations if they succeeded in getting people on benefit back to work. However, the scheme was not as successful as first hoped. As Jill Sherman reported in the Times (24/5/12), it failed to get enough sick and disabled people back to work and some of the organisations found themselves in financial difficulty.

By 2012, three charities that had contracts had pulled out of the programme and a fourth, Groundwork South West, a voluntary skills organisation, had entered administration.

Poor IT systems, Jobcentres' failure to refer clients and a high number of appeals against medical assessments were all being blamed.

Mr Duncan-Smith originally told the 18 prime contractors that about 30 per cent of referrals would be those claiming Incapacity Benefit (Employment Support Allowance). But in the nine months after the programme started only 7 per cent of clients had fallen into this "harder to help" category, while the rest were on jobseeker's allowance. Some companies were losing hundreds of thousands of pounds each year because of the shortfall.

Philip Curry, policy manager at the Employment Related Services Association, which represented the contractors, said they had been expecting to receive 180,000 clients in the year on higher premiums. "In reality only 40,000 long-term sick clients were referred to the 18 contractors and more than 500,000 people on jobseeker's allowance," he said. Of all those referred, only one in four had found work, much lower than the government target of 36 per cent.

The shortage of the more vulnerable clients was partly because of medical assessments carried out for all new claimants of ESA and those still on incapacity benefit. The government had claimed that 60 per cent of people tested would be found fit for work but the assessments for more than 2.7 million claimants of Incapacity Benefit took longer to carry out because of a shortage of doctors.

Many of those found fit to work appealed. "Forty per cent of those who have completed work tests have appealed and forty per cent of those have been successful," said Matthew Lester, director of operations for Papworth Trust, a voluntary organisation working with disabled people.

In 2012-13 the government asked Atos Healthcare to carry out an assessment of the physical capacity of those claiming incapacity benefit or ESA. In March 2013, figures from the Department of Work and Pensions showed that 878,000 people dropped their claims rather than face an examination. This was more than a third of those receiving the benefit. 1.44 million were assessed of whom 55 per cent were judged fit for immediate work and 23.9 per cent able to do some level of work. The DWP's figures showed however that 38 per cent of appeals against the assessment's findings were successful. The cost to the taxpayer of incorrect assessments was £20 million a year.

DWP statistics published on 22nd January 2014 said that more than 8 out of 10 incapacity benefit claimants were establishing entitlement to employment and support allowance (ESA). Focusing on claims referred for reassessment between January 2013 and March 2013, the new figures highlighted that 84 per cent of completed reassessments resulted in entitlement to ESA, with 34 per cent placed in the work-related activity group (WRAG) and 51 per cent in the support group.

In March 2014, figures released by the DWP[*] showed that between April and June 2013, 31 per cent of completed work capability assessments (WCA's) had found the claimant 'fit for work'.

---

[*] 'Employment and Support Allowance: Outcomes of Work Capability Assessments, Great Britain'.

The statistical release also showed that 69 per cent of claimants with an outcome for their claim were entitled to employment and support allowance and that, within this, 18 per cent were placed in the work-related activity group and 51 per cent in the support group, whilst 31 per cent were assessed as 'fit to work'.

According to leaked memos in the summer of 2014, the cost of ESA was projected to rise significantly. The memos revealed a range of options for reducing costs, but concluded that there appeared to be "not much low-hanging fruit left".

"This leaves us vulnerable to a breach [of the cap]", said one memo. A spokesman for the DWP said the memos were simply hypothetical plans for different scenarios, not official forecasts.

Dame Anne Begg, the Chair of the Work and Pensions Select Committee, said the government had been over estimating the number of people on incapacity benefits that were able to work, risking a breach of the self-imposed welfare cap.

She said "Employment Support Allowance has tightened the criteria but what they've actually discovered, lo and behold, instead of lots of people languishing on incapacity benefit, they've found that these people, when they've re-assessed them, are very ill or disabled."

While a key aim of the benefit is to get people off welfare and into work, people are moving onto ESA which has fewer sanctions – when someone's benefit is stopped for misconduct – than Jobseeker's Allowance, the memo said.

Statistics released by the DWP in November 2014 showed that in the period from 3rd December 2012 – when the new ESA sanctions regime was introduced – to June 2014, the total number of adverse sanction decisions was 49,047 and of these 8,009 were applied for failure to attend a mandatory interview, while 41,051 were applied for failure to participate in work related activity.

The statistics also showed that 31,728 case decisions were reviewed of which 16,835 were overturned while 493 were appealed (of which 149 were overturned).

The cost of incapacity benefit remained high. According to Treasury figures published in the Times (7/7/15), it cost the government £14.8 bn in 2015/16.

Some of those sanctioned were concerned that this might affect their housing benefit. In a bulletin published on the 14th August 2014 the DWP reported that 'although the majority of these notifications have no impact on the housing benefit entitlement, claims are being suspended while further enquiries are made. This in turn is creating additional work for the local authority as they have to check every notification to see whether the claimant is no longer entitled to benefit or benefit has ceased due to a sanction.' As a result, the DWP said that it had introduced the interim solution of instructing staff to advise claimants to contact their local authority when sanctioned. Those sanctioned and deprived of ESA should not necessarily be denied housing benefit. In December 2014, the Social Security Advisory Committee (SSAC) launched a consultation on the government's proposal to close a 'loophole' relating to employment and support allowance (ESA) repeat claims. The government believed that some people were exploiting the current system which allows claimants to make another claim six months after being refused benefit and that it intends to close down this 'loophole' by making it clear that from 30th March 2015 anyone seeking to make a repeat claim to ESA after they have been found to have limited capability for work will need to produce medical evidence indicating a deterioration in an existing health condition or the onset of a new condition. ESA would not be paid to claimants in these circumstances pending an appeal.

Figures released on 27th August 2015 in response to a Freedom of Information (FoI) request showed that some 2,380 people had died (around 90 a month) between December 2011 and February 2014, after having been found to be fit for work and no longer eligible to receive the ESA.

So the war goes on between our political leaders and State employees on one side and the possibly but not certainly too ill to work on the other side. Citizens of this country should know about this sad war and we should build a better society in which there is no such war going on.

10. Disability Living Allowance (Personal Independence Payment)

Purpose

Those who have difficulty in the ordinary process of living (not necessarily working) and who may need help from others have had a special non means tested allowance designed to help them live a reasonable life in spite of their health problems or disability. It has had two components – mobility allowance and care allowance – and each has been assessed according to the person's disability.   For the care component there are three levels of disability and for the mobility component two levels. It has been awarded either indefinitely or for a fixed period. The number of people claiming it rose steadily after it was introduced in 1992 and by 2006 there were 2.8m people receiving it (Times 07/10/06), two thirds of whom received it indefinitely. By 2012, there were 3.3 million people receiving the benefit.

Abuse

However, there had long been concern that some able-bodied citizens were fraudulently claiming the benefit. In June 2006 for instance Keith Jones, a professional boxer who had fought nearly 100 contests while claiming the allowance for chronic asthma, was found guilty of benefit fraud.

Government reaction to abuse

David Blunkett, the Secretary of State for Work and Pensions in the Labour government had expressed concern at the ease with which disability living allowance could be claimed fraudulently and had launched a crackdown.

Mr Duncan-Smith, Secretary of State for Work and Pensions in the coalition government from 2010, decided to change the emphasis of the benefit by calling it the Personal Independent Payment (PIP) and the new basis of payment was planned to begin in October 2013. Previously, for instance, someone not able to walk for 50 metres qualified for the benefit but under the new system only someone unable to walk for 20 metres qualified.

The full implementation had been planned for October 2013 but in the event the programme was not ready all over the country by this date. So only a few areas of Britain had to adopt the new system. The rest were expected to join later.

The results of an assessment were made available by the government in February 2014. These showed that only 37 per cent of standard claims for PIP had been successful. Almost two out of three people who tried to claim the new disability benefit were rejected after medical tests.

Ministers claimed that the new benefit, which followed face-to-face assessment and regular interviews, would lead to more accurate awards and save hundreds of millions of pounds. The government expected 600,000 fewer claimants to receive the benefit by 2018. In January 2014, the DWP issued a new information bulletin to remind local authority housing benefit staff about the further roll out of Personal Independence Payment (PIP) from the 4th February 2014.

The DWP advised that whilst new claims for PIP were being made across Great Britain, the new benefit was being rolled out to existing claimants of

Disability Living Allowance (DLA) in specific 'reassessment' areas in different parts of the country.

Criticism of government action

Critics however argued that disabled people would lose out in many ways as a result of the government's welfare reform. According to the work by the Demos think-tank for the disability charity Scope, disabled people would lose £28 billion by 2018 under a series of benefit cuts and thousands would be hit by as many as six cuts at the same time, losing up to £4,600. 3.7 million disabled people would be affected by the cuts with an estimated 3,000 people hit by six separate cuts and 12,500 by five. "What's shocking is that the government doesn't assess the likely combined impact of these changes, only the impact of each change individually" said Claudia Wood, Deputy Director of Demos. But a spokesman for the Department of Work and Pensions (as reported in The Times 28/3/14) said the report was scaremongering. "This government is committed to supporting disabled people and we continue to spend around £50 billion a year on disabled people" he said.

In June 2014 (reported in The Times 20/6/14) the Public Accounts Committee of the House of Commons found that the new welfare scheme for PIP to replace Disability Living Allowance was a 'fiasco'. They found that thousands of sick and disabled people had to wait more than six months to be awarded disability benefits because of a backlog of more than 780,000 claims. Personal Independence Payments had been introduced by the government in 2013. The new payments were awarded only after face-to-face assessments but these often were delayed or cancelled. This had forced many to turn to loans, charitable donations or food banks to make ends meet.

The MP's said it was "alarming" that terminally ill people had been waiting for a month for a decision, rather than the 10 day target, while other claimants had been waiting more than 26 weeks. They argued that the failure of the Department for Work and Pensions to pilot the scheme meant that basic assumptions on how long the assessments would take had not been tested. "The personal stories we heard were shocking" said Margaret Hodge, the committee chairwoman. "We heard evidence of a claimant requiring hospital intervention as a result of the stress caused by the delays suffered".

In April 2013 the DWP started accepting new claims for the payment in northern England but had made only 360 decisions when the scheme was extended nationwide in June. Margaret Hodge said that "the DWP has let down some of the most vulnerable people in our society, many of whom have had to wait more than six months for their claims to be decided".

The cross-party committee accused Atos, which held the contract, of providing "incorrect and potentially misleading" information about its capabilities when tendering to carry out assessments for the government. A spokesman for the Disability Benefits Consortium said that it was still inundated with calls from people waiting more than a year to receive a decision.

On the 17th December 2014, DWP statistics were released showing that almost 240,000 claims for personal independence payment (PIP) were awaiting a decision. They also showed that for the period from April 2013 to 31st October 2014 more than 46,000 disability living allowance reassessments still had to be cleared.

592,000 new claims had been registered for PIP, of which 24,500 were claims made under the special rules for terminally ill people. 76,300 disability living allowance (DLA) reassessments had been registered for PIP, of which 900 were claims made under the special rules. 352,100 new claims had been cleared (i.e. a decision had been made or the claim had been withdrawn) of which 28,700 were for claims made under the special rules. 29,900 reassessments had been cleared, of which 1,100 were for claims made under the special rules.

The cost of disability living allowance (or PIP) was given as £15.6 bn in Treasury figures published in the Times (9/7/15) while attendance allowance cost £5.5 bn.

More cases of abuse

However, cases of abuse continue.

For example, Channel 5 in one of its 'Benefits' programmes (January 2015) covered the use by a mildly disabled man of a car, most of the cost of which had been met by the state.

Another example was reported in The Times (6/2/15). Alan Bannister 54, was found guilty of fraudulently claiming benefits for disability living allowance to the tune of £26,000. After claiming his arthritis made it too painful for him to walk, he further claimed funding for a car from a mobility scheme. He was caught red-handed, when the DWP filmed him playing golf at a competitive event for over 4 and a half hours. It also transpired that he had a golf handicap of 6, was the club champion and had won several tournaments. He was tried before a jury and found guilty.

Surely a system that can lead to such expensive fraud at the taxpayer's expense can not be right? But we, through our elected representatives, are responsible for the system.

The truth is that government is just no good at making arrangements which are both publicly funded and a help to people in need. Their services must be provided in some other way. The state should be arbiter not provider. How that can be done is explained in Part II.

But it is not all about money. What is more important is that wherever possible the disabled can be helped to live useful lives.

A positive approach to the disabled

Most people want to do something worth while with their lives and if they are judged to be disabled they are given the money but not helped to make a contribution to society. Following a remark by Lord Freud, a number of people wrote to the Times (17/10/14) to show how the disabled can be helped to do this. Mark Macnair, Emeritus Professor at Exeter University wrote: 'Twenty years ago, I was in charge of the University of Exeter's research greenhouses and we agreed with social services to use their severely disabled clients, who were being trained in horticulture, for mundane jobs such as pot washing. We could not afford to pay them at a university rate but we gave them as much as they could receive without losing benefits. The clients were given self-respect and we had our pots washed. It is logical to suggest that the severely disabled should be facilitated to participate in the job market at a rate lower than the national minimum wage – as other countries recognise'.

Parents wrote to say how the opportunity for making some contribution would help their disabled children. Glenda Stock wrote: 'My adult son has learning difficulties. He loves work but always needs supervision. He lives happily in supported living; he fills his week by voluntary work and paying to do various activities which are funded by social services. If he could earn £2 per hour he would feel valued. Any low wage would have to be flexible as there are many degrees of disability but such a scheme would help my son.' Gordon Muir wrote: 'Sir, I would be delighted to see my autistic son in a position that brought him self-worth and happiness. There may be extraordinary costs associated with such work – if an employer were forced to absorb those then there may be no job.' George Flint found good practice in Spain: 'While visiting a university in Spain I was greeted by a woman with Down's syndrome, who meticulously issued my visitor's pass. Later I found that her wages were subsidised by the government.'

Many disabled people are at the moment denied the opportunity to live a useful life. We should aim to enable the disabled to make some useful contribution and to be paid for it as well as receiving monetary support.

In June 2015, as reported by the BBC (5/6/15) the High Court ruled that a delay in paying welfare benefits to two disabled people was unlawful.

Delays of at least nine months for Personal Independence Payments (PIPs) for these "most vulnerable" of people were unreasonable, a judge ruled. But the court ruled the pair's human rights were not breached, which meant that they were not entitled to compensation.

At the time there were 78,000 people waiting to hear if they could claim PIPs. Of these 3,200 had waited more than a year to have their claims processed and 22,800 had waited for more than 20 weeks.

The claimants, known only as Ms C and Mr W, said the delays meant they struggled to pay for food and fuel and this caused their health to decline. Ms C, from Kent, who has ME, severe depression and other health problems, waited from September 2013 to October 2014 to have her eligibility assessed. The court heard she lived a "hand-to-mouth" existence, spending £8 per week on food and only left her home once a week to visit the supermarket. In her judgement, Mrs Justice Patterson said Ms C was required to travel some distance for face-to-face PIP assessments despite the fact she had "explained her difficulty in travelling".

Ms C said she could not travel and was told her application would be cancelled, causing her "considerable stress and anxiety" but PIPs were eventually granted based on 'phone and paper evidence.

Mr W, who was a carpenter until he contracted ulcerative colitis in 2013 and had his colon removed, waited from February to December 2014 for a PIP decision.

The Department for Work and Pensions (DWP) had agreed the delays were unacceptable but argued they were not unlawful and said more than 800 extra staff were assigned to work on PIPs after problems emerged.

Note that this is another 800 people to be paid by the state in addition to thousands more being trained by the state to operate the benefit system at a cost of more than £200 billion a year.

11. Legal Aid

Legal Aid is not administered as part of the social security system but is in fact a benefit. The state since 1949 has met the cost of legal support for those who are considered not to be able to afford it.

The support is means-tested and so basically unfair. Someone who earns £x pcm is considered eligible for support but someone earning £x +5 may not be eligible. It is alleged that only the rich and the poor can afford to go to court.

This cost the state more than £2 bn in 2010.

The coalition government therefore decided to reduce the cost by refusing to provide financial support in certain circumstances such as family disputes, for which financial support fell by 80% in 2014.

Some lawyers have agreed to help clients without a fee but many have protested at this reduction of support arguing that it undermines the principle that all should be equal before the law.

B.   What's wrong with the system? - Summary

1. National insurance deeply flawed

In theory, each individual employee and the employer must contribute a fixed sum while the self-employed people contribute a different sum.   In return, those who contributed were entitled to receive a range of benefits, such as the basic state pension, unemployment pay (Jobseeker's Allowance) and statutory sick pay.   In a proper insurance system, the revenue being paid to the institution must be sufficient to meet that institution's expected expenditure. Insurance contributions could have been invested in a fund from which, in due course, payments would be made on such occasions and in such sums as set out in an original contract.   Instead, national insurance contributions (NIC) are kept by the government which allocated, in 2014, one fifth to the NHS while keeping the remainder in the National Insurance Fund, from which payments can be made towards the cost of social security such as pensions and incapacity benefit.

They have, in practice, been treated as a tax while payments have been made from government funds: 'pay as you go'.   So government did not have to increase National Insurance contributions to finance higher expenditure on social security and in practice there was no proper relationship between contributions and benefits.

The absurdity of the way the system worked was well illustrated in a letter from Alison Clark published in The Times (13/1/09).

"I have received notification from the department of Work and Pensions", she wrote, "that I am not entitled to Jobseeker's Allowance as I have not paid sufficient Class 1 national insurance contributions (NIC) over the past two years. Having been employed on a part or full-time basis since the age of 12, claimed no benefits other than three months' unemployment benefit and having no children, yet paying higher rate income tax for the past 21 years plus full NIC for 30 years, I was a little bewildered as, surely, I must be a vast net contributor to the state. Apparently the self-employed person's payment for Class 2 and 4 contributions doesn't count toward eligibility for Jobseeker's Allowance. Interestingly, I also received a separate notification that as I have now paid 30 years NIC I have paid for my pension, payable at 65, but must keep on paying NIC while I continue to work."

Ed Milliband in a speech in June 2014 made the same point.

"How many times have we heard people say - "for years and years, I paid in and then when the time came and I needed help I got nothing out.""

Rewarding contribution was a key principle of the Beveridge Report and it is a key intuition of the British people. But it is a principle that has been forgotten by governments of both major parties.

In 2013/14 national insurance contributions (NICs) were the second largest source of government revenue, raising an estimated £105 bn, slightly more than the total for VAT receipts. Income tax revenue raised amounted to an estimated £156 bn. To most employees, NIC's are indistinguishable from a tax on earnings while governments have not relied on NIC's in determining levels of payment.

It is not surprising therefore that in 2014 the Chancellor of the Exchequer started to consider merging NICs and taxes. Putting together these separate charges would make clearer to taxpayers how much they hand over to government and it would simplify administration.

According to The Times (30/6/14), under a merger of the two charges, the total amount paid by workers on the basic rate of income tax would rise from 20 per cent to 32 per cent. The amount paid by those in the higher bracket would rise from 40 per cent to about 52 per cent.

A survey in 2012 by the Institute of Directors found that 79 per cent of businesses backed the idea of merging income tax with national insurance to reduce their administrative burdens.

There were fears however that the move would involve merging two computer systems and could cause another Whitehall IT disaster. Concerns over the software caused Mr Osborne to pull back from an announcement in April 2014 according to informed sources.

"We came within a whisker of doing this at the last budget but in the end we decided against it", a source said. "They are currently on two separate computer systems and we thought the risk was just too great. But it's something we could do in the next parliament."

The merger would be honest and efficient but it would put the state duly in control and the principle of personal responsibility through insurance would be abandoned, a move in the wrong direction.

2. *Escalating Costs*

Social security expenditure has risen much more than originally envisaged. Increased unemployment in the 1970's and 1980's, increased expectation of life and changes in social habits, such as the increasing number of lone-parent households, have all contributed to an escalation of costs. Moreover the increased standard of living enjoyed by most people in employment raised the expectation of higher benefits for those in need. But costs the government could afford in times of full employment were harder to meet when the economy languished.

According to George Osborne and Ian Duncan-Smith, as reported in the Sunday Times (21/6/15), the Labour government of 1997 – 2010 "allowed the cost of our welfare state to spiral by a startling 30%". The introduction of tax credits was one of the major causes of this.

So working-age benefits had by 2010 reached £94 bn and the total package reached between £210 and £220 bn pa. Working age benefits had risen from 8% of public spending in 1980 to 13% in 2014.

The coalition government formed in 2010 was determined to reduce costs and in March 2014 the House of Commons agreed a 2015-16 welfare cap of £119.5 bn, excluding the state pension and some unemployment benefits.

According to Georgia Graham, Political Correspondent at the Daily Telegraph (20/6/14) the government's self-imposed welfare spending cap could be breached because of the huge cost of people moving off Jobseeker's Allowance on to Sickness Benefit. In this case Ministers must explain to parliament if the government breaches its own limit on welfare spending and will have to ask MPs to approve additional spending.

The government did reduce welfare spending after 2012 and in June 2015 George Osborne confirmed that there would be a cut of £12 bn in the 2015-20 period. On the other hand David Cameron has refused to cut pensioner benefit and does not support a cut in child benefit. Once the welfare budget grows so large political leaders are worried that cuts in it will lose vital votes. Such a connection undermines the justice of the welfare system.

Even so, George Osborne and Ian Duncan-Smith, in their Sunday Times article, commented that the Office for Budget Responsibility (OBR) has forecast that working age benefits would be 12.7% of spending in 2019-20.

3a) *Failure of the State to meet expectations: benefits too low*

The provision of benefits in return for NIC was the responsibility of the state and there was no higher authority to force the state to live up to the expectations of citizens. Pensions for the old had, in the 1970's, risen each year in line with earnings. The Thatcher government decided that to continue such a practice would, in view of the growth of earnings, be too costly. The Labour party in opposition opposed this change but after taking power took some time before it was prepared to bring back the former system. In any case, earnings-related benefits would have to be met by earning-related NIC and/or higher taxes.

3b) *Delay in payments of benefits*

Many people entitled to benefit have alleged that it is the delay in payment of benefit which causes much difficulty for them. A cross party report, backed by the Church of England stated that this was the biggest reason given for referral to food banks (Times 15/12/14).

3c) *Too many people on low income*

What is more serious is that many benefits go to people in work simply because they are not paid enough. As Janice Turner wrote in an article in the Times (4/11/14) retail workers are frequently being paid just the minimum wage (£6.50 ph in 2015). A Unite summary of Sainsbury employees in 2013 found that 60% relied on working tax credits to top up their wages.

Food bills increased by 44% in the last decade and energy costs have doubled but wages have not picked up in the same way. By late 2014 5.2 million people were being paid less than the rate which Janice Turner believed to be necessary to live a decent life (£7.65 ph for the UK and 7,80 in London).

So long as wages are low, the state has to pay out benefits, costing £28m pa to enable low earners to live a reasonable life. But how much better and simpler it would be for the 5m low paid people to be paid at least £9 ph so that the whole wasteful procedure of working out benefits can be avoided.

If the problems of the welfare state are to be overcome the first step must be the higher minimum wage. This is the context which justifies the Chancellor of the Exchequer's plan to raise the Minimum Wage to £9 ph by 2020.

More than 700 companies, according to Janice Turner, have signed up to the living wage but in retail, which has the biggest proportion of low paid workers, not a single high street name had signed up (although John Lewis shares its profits among staff).

4. Means testing (or targeting)

Universal benefits such as the basic state pension (until the 1990's) or Child Benefit are straight forward but, if such benefits are all raised to a good standard , this is a great cost to the taxpayer. Some have argued, therefore, that money should be targeted on those in need.

Why should the rich family get benefit just to buy the odd luxuries? Surely it would be better to give it to poor families.

The result is means-testing. The state has to check on the income, capital and responsibilities of people in order to find out if they are poor enough to receive a payment. Applicants have to complete often lengthy forms to support their case. The state must then check that there is no abuse.

Targeting is also inefficient, costly and resource intensive. Administration costs eat up to 10 per cent of means-tested Income Support but (until the introduction of the Minimum Income Guarantee) only 1 per cent of the basic state pension, a universal benefit.

The injustices and complexities of means-testing have been illustrated in the criticisms above of the pension credit, income support, housing and council tax benefit and tax credits. Means-tested benefits are, moreover, in many cases unclaimed by those who are entitled to them. Yet means-testing has been increasingly used in the 21st century.

5. Vulnerability to fraud

As shown above, there are many ways in which dishonest people can secure benefits to which they are not entitled: by claiming Job Seeker's Allowance while still working for cash for instance or by failing to reveal certain income and thus qualifying for means-tested benefits such as income support and pension credit.

In spite of hard punishments meted out to those found out, social security fraud has become commonplace because it seems so easy. The integrity of ordinary people is undermined. The Hunts Post (11/12/03) reported several cases coming before local magistrates in December 2003. Tina Cary and Nigel Lovitt of Beauchamp Close in Eaton Socon pleaded guilty to failing to declare that Miss Carey was operating a child minding business while claiming housing and council tax benefits. The court heard payments totalling £6,104 were made between 2001 and 2003. Investigation officers from the council's benefits section discovered the fraud while making routine enquiries. Rebecca Thomson, formerly of Humberdale Way, Warboys, pleaded guilty to failing to declare that she had a job between 2001 and 2002. Miss Thompson was overpaid housing benefit and council tax benefit of £1,928.

Much of the fraud has been on a very large scale. The Cambridge Evening News (11/11/05) reported how a Mrs Joanne Fitzpatrick had been sent for sentence at the Crown Court by magistrates at Huntingdon after she admitted six offences of making false representations to get benefits. Fitzpatrick had been overpaid about £32,000 - £21,000 in income support, £9,200 in housing benefit and £1,500 in Council Tax benefit.

The Times (10/12/04) reported how a lady called Julie Cane enjoyed the lifestyle of a millionaire, with staff and gardeners at her £1.6 million country mansion at Cowley in West London and nanny care for her seven children. But as far as the benefit office was concerned, the divorcee was living in a modest two-bedroom terrace housing association property in Uxbridge. The deceit enabled her to secure £127,612.20 from social services.

In February 2009 (Times 24/2/09) Swansea Crown Court dealt with Shashi Bacheta, 52 and Jeffrey Cole, 58, who went sailing aboard a £100,000 yacht while falsely claiming benefit. Bacheta was claiming housing benefit, council tax relief, income support and disability living allowance totalling about £40,000 after claiming that she was unable to dress or feed herself. Investigators discovered that Bacheta was working as a postmistress at the Rheidol Avenue Post Office in Swansea while Cole, the sub-postmaster, ran the newsagent side of the business. Cole claimed around £12,000 while pretending to be Bacheta's landlord.

Surely there must be something wrong with a system that allows one person to practice fraud on such a scale? Why do British people put up with such a system?

Much fraud is simply treated as error. According to Mark Heath, a fraud lawyer at Watson Burton, quoted in the Times (29/1/08), only a third of fraud is detected: "It is easier to describe fraud as an error. A lot of cases where money is trying to be claimed back are fraud, but it is easier to settle and say it is a mistake."

According to figures issued by the Department for Work and Pensions issued in February 2007 (Times 13/2/07) £770m was estimated to have been overpaid in Housing Benefit, of which £140m was due to fraud, £190m to official error and £440m to customer error.

In June 2010 , Zahid Ali, a consultant to the NTU was jailed for 9 months after admitting seven counts of benefit fraud (Times 23/6/10). He lived in a gated Surrey home worth £1 million while claiming housing benefit for two properties owned by his wife. Zahid Ali earned £325 a hour as a consultant but took half day holidays to sign on for Job Seeker's Allowance. He failed to declare earnings of £212,000 between 2004 and 2008 while making claims for various benefits from Sutton Council, Reigate Council, Banstead Council and the DWP.

By 2013, benefit fraud, including tax credit fraud, was estimated at £2 billion p.a. and in September, Keir Starmer Director of Public Prosecutions launched a major crackdown on such dishonesty (Times 16/9/13). Previously, benefit cheats had been charged under social security legislation carrying a maximum sentence of seven years. After 2013 they could be charged under the Fraud Act and could face 10 years in prison.

Benefit frauds of less than £20,000 had been automatically tried in magistrates' courts, which could only sentence people to up to 12 months imprisonment for multiple offences. For a single offence, the maximum was six months.

On the 6th November 2013, a programme on BBC 1, 'Britain on the Fiddle', gave some examples of fraud. In Stoke, a woman who won £95,000 on a game show continued to claim Income Support, Housing Benefit, single-person discount on her Council Tax and free school meals. In Croydon, a convicted benefits fraudster was given 6 months to pay back £1 million or go back to prison and in Kensington and Chelsea, a man who had already fleeced the benefit system of £90,000 continued to claim disability benefit in two names while running a house clearance business.

These incidents illustrate the incapacity of the state to administer fairly and efficiently the arrangement for boosting income. It is also fair to admit that some people who would not steal from their neighbour are happy to steal from the state out of social security provisions.

Fraud & error

Official statistics showed that the total estimated value of overpayments due to fraud and error across all benefits in 2012/2013 was £3.5 billion. In January 2014 the Work and Pensions Committee announced an enquiry into fraud and error in the benefits system. The enquiry would investigate where errors occur in the benefits system and the adequacy of steps being taken to reduce them, including: internal DWP processes, communications and joint working between departments and local authorities, including through the single DWP Fraud and Error Service and communication with claimants. They would also consider approaches to tackling benefit fraud, including: the proposed Single Fraud Investigation Service, steps designed to discourage fraudulent claims and identify potentially fraudulent claims at the earliest possible stage and the recently announced 'Benefits: are you doing the right thing?' campaign.

The implications of fraud and error for the introduction of universal credit would also be examined as well as in other welfare reforms, including the risks of online fraud and lessons to be learned from the private sector, including online fraud protection and data protection issues.

On the 14th May 2015, the DWP released statistics on 'Fraud and Error in the benefit system' for 2014/2015. This showed that while overall fraud and error amounted to 1.9 per cent of total expenditure (down from 2.1 per cent in 2013/2014), for housing benefit it amounted to 5.7 per cent of total expenditure.

According to the new figures, of the total £3.2bn that was overpaid, claimant error overpayments were at 0.8 per cent of expenditure, or £1.3bn, official error overpayments were at 0.4 per cent of expenditure, or

£0.7bn and fraud overpayments were at 0.7 per cent of expenditure, or £1.1bn.

The report also highlighted that 0.9 per cent of total expenditure was underpaid (the same percentage as in 2013/2014) – equating to £1.4bn – of which 0.6 per cent (or £0.9bn) was due to claimant error and 0.3 per cent (or £0.5bn) to official error.

Incredible stories of fraud continued to appear. As reported in the Times (8/7/15) a self-styled Austro-Hungarian aristocrat avoided jail after being convicted of fraudulently claiming more than £18,000 in benefits, having argued that there was no one else who could look after her cats. Vera-Brigitte Bilek Von Sternberg, who asked to be referred to variously as Lady or Countess, claimed £18,767 in housing and council tax benefit over three years from Kensington and Chelsea council in London, despite simultaneously renting out her £1.1 million house in Chelsea to four tenants.

6. *Effect on family unit*

The family unit is being undermined by the benefit system. A man and a woman marry and have a child. One parent works and earns enough to pay tax. They all live together in one house. Another man and woman have a child. The mother and baby live together as a one-parent household and receive state benefits. The father lives elsewhere and, under pressure from the Child Support Agency (CSA), may contribute to the upkeep of the child but not sufficiently to prevent the mother being dependent on the state. The parents who behave responsibly pay to support those in need because of the irresponsibility of one or both of the other parents.

Another problem arises from the government's apparent belief that working is more important than bringing up a family and its consequent readiness to pay for some of the childcare of working mothers. Where parents regard the upbringing of their children as the most important consideration, the mother (or father sometimes) may opt to be at home all the time while they have any children who are under 5 and after that only work when this does not prevent their being at home to welcome the children back from school. Such parents do not have childcare costs and therefore no state handout. Next door, the main earner has the same income as does the single earner in the first household but the second parent also works, if only part-time, so they incur childcare costs which the state may subsidise. The quality of society depends on the qualities of its citizens and this depends (probably more than on anything else) on how they are brought up by their parents. Yet the state gives money to those who leave their young children in order to work but not to those who look after them themselves.

This point also applies to maternity benefit now payable for 12 months to all mothers who are having a baby but plan to go back to work. If the mother does not propose to go back to work, she does not get any such benefit. This is basically unfair, discriminating against the mother who stays to home to look after the children.

A report from the Centre for Policy Studies, 'The Price of Parenthood' written by Jill Kirby and published in January 2005, illustrates the way in which parents who split up or never marry may receive considerable state benefits financed by taxpayer parents who jointly bring up their children.

The report argues that the system of means-tested tax credits and benefits acts as a perverse incentive for couples to split up or not to get married. Jill Kirby concludes "that this is grossly unfair on low and middle income married couples who work hard and who stay together, because it forces them to subsidise workless lone parents. It also acts as a disincentive for middle-income married couples to have children."

Paying out money for the good of the community is fine but the benefits to single parents foster a system in which children are increasingly denied what is most important to them, being brought up in a home with their mother and father.

A further study by the Marriage Foundation was conducted in 2013 and summarised by Nicholas Heller in the Sunday Times (15/9/13). This study found a discrepancy of 240,000 between the ONS figures on the number of lone-parent households in England and Wales and the number of people in receipt of single parent benefits.

In other words some 240,000 people were claiming to live apart and to receive benefit but were really living together.

Harry Benson, the report's author said: "It is indefensible that parents in committed, stable relationships face such significant penalties for staying together, to the extent that some pretend to be separated to avoid them. Those couples who have not made the decision to commit to each other will be strongly dissuaded from doing so by the tax system. It is irresponsible for the government to continue this disincentive to make relationships work. They should be striving to encourage solid relationships, which are key to avoiding expensive social problems further down the line."

7. Complexity

The British social security system is now so complex that only a very few people understand it in its entirety.

For all means-tested benefits, in particular, the amount people are entitled to receive will often depend on the details of their income and commitments. Civil Servants have to work out precisely what a person should get in the knowledge that if they get it wrong and if the person complains to the media and it is reported there will be problems! There must therefore be senior civil servants to whom problems can be referred. Computers are fully employed making the calculation but the accuracy of their work depends of course on the accuracy of the input. So, increasing complexity leads to ever increasing administration and costs.

The complexity of rules governing social security has led to increasing use of computerised systems. Problems are significant, bearing in mind the following conclusion drawn by the report 'A Recipe for Rip-offs: Time for a new approach' by the Public Administration Select Committee of the House of Commons (18/7/11):

'Government IT does not have a happy history. The last 10 years have seen several failed attempts at reform. The current government seems determined to succeed where others have failed and we are greatly encouraged by its progress to date. However, numerous challenges remain and fundamentally transforming how Government uses IT will require departments to engage more directly with innovative firms, to integrate technology into policy-making and reform how they develop their systems. The fundamental requirement is that Government needs the right skills, knowledge and capacity in-house to deliver these changes. Without the ability to engage with IT suppliers as an intelligent customer – able to secure the most efficient deal and benchmark its costs – and to understand the role technology can play in the delivery of public services, Government is doomed to repeat the mistakes of the past.'

A complex structure needs complex technology. But why does social security have to be complex? Surely we should have a system which is clear and easy for ordinary people to understand.

8. Damaging effects of the benefits system on the quality of British society

The worst aspect of the benefits system is probably its harmful effect on British society.

a.) Creation of dependency

The welfare state was born of a noble vision: that everyone should have sufficient means but remain a free, self-reliant person with a sense of independence. In return for national insurance contributions from themselves, the employer if appropriate and with some support from the state, a national insurance would be created from which in unemployment, ill health or old age they could draw out the income needed for their basic physical needs without any sense of dependency or official prying into their affairs.

Sadly the system has deteriorated to such an extent that more people than ever are in some way dependent upon the state, having to reveal their income and capital so that officials can work out how big a handout they should receive.

One depressing result of the benefit system has been the creation of state-dependent families where children, parents and grand-parents live on benefits from the state.

In the Sunday Times (25/7/10) Margaret Driscott and Kevin Dawling gave the McFadden family from Ellesmere Port, as an example:

'Neither Sue McFadden nor two of her three daughters, all single mothers bringing up six children between them, nor McFadden's oldest grandson, Kyle, were in work. The family was living on benefits of more than £32,000 a year with no prospect of supporting itself.

In 2012 there were believed to be some 120,000 problem families, each on average costing the state £75,000. On the 17th August 2014 the Sunday Times described how some of these families lived and how much they cost the state. Neither the author nor the reader would have wanted to belong to such a family. Nor would we want to be parents of children living on benefits in this way.

Yet the state allows millions of people to depend on benefits. We should all be ashamed of the way our country treats its citizens. What we should do is to help all adults to be responsible citizens, able to run their own lives. The creation of dependency is not the fault of the dependants, it is the fault of the governments we elect. We must work out a better policy.

An independent responsible person will ensure that he has sufficient savings to be available in difficult times. The UK benefits system undermines this as people expect that the state will provide money when they are in need, so feel it unnecessary to save when times are good.

b.) Benefit Ghettos

A report by the Centre for Social Justice in May 2013 was summarised by David Leppard in the Sunday Times (19/5/13). The report showed that parts of Britain had become "benefit ghettos" where more than half the working-age residents depended on out-of-work benefits. Some areas of Denbighshire in north Wales, Birmingham, Blackburn, Wirral, Lincolnshire and Essex top a league table of welfare black spots where worklessness is "entrenched".

The Centre for Social Justice identified 70 neighbourhoods in Liverpool where the number of people claiming out-of-work benefits was 30 per cent or more. This was followed by Birmingham with 49 such neighbourhoods, Hull with 45, Manchester with 40 and Leeds with 37.

According to Christian Guy, the Centre's managing director, "people in these neighbourhoods have been constantly written off as incapable and their poverty plight as inevitable. Their lives have been limited by a fatalistic assumption that they have little prospect of anything better."

The study found that 1.8 million British children - one in five – were growing up in a home where no one had a job. This is the second highest rate in Europe.

One charity, Chance UK, said that some children did not even understand what work was. Asked what they wanted to be when they grew up, the children said "I want to be famous" or that they wanted to be the "boss" of a gang.

For 9.6 million families – 30 per cent of all families – benefits made up more than half of their entire income.

Worryingly, the Centre for Social Justice says that unemployment had become "intergenerational" in some areas, with grandparents, parents and working-age children all being out of work.

It identified Rhyl in Benbighshire, a dilapidated Victorian seaside resort, as having the highest level of out-of-work dependency. In the town's west end, 67 per cent aged between 16 and 64 were on out-of-work benefits.

The second worst "welfare ghetto" identified in the report was Brandwood in Birmingham, a run-down area on the southern fringes of Britain's second biggest city. Here 60 per cent of the working-age population were on welfare.

But the huge cost is not the main problem that the benefit system created. More terrible is the fact that large numbers of people never had the opportunity to make a contribution through their work for the good of society.

"Troubled families"

The coalition government on the basis of uncertain statistics, concluded in 2012 that there were some 66,100 households containing troubled families where there might be 3 generations almost all receiving benefit for some reason or other and in April 2012 a special programme was launched to help members of these families find work and get off benefits.

In September 2014 the DWP published a report on this programme for April 2012 to July 2014. This showed that 76,000 individuals in 66,100 households had been identified on the DWP's systems as having been on the troubled families programme and in receipt of an out of work benefit since the programme stared in April 2012.

c.) System seen as unfair to society as a whole

According to a report from the Centre for Policy Studies published in October 2012 (based on the figures for 2010/2011 and reviewed by Jack Grimstone in the Sunday Times 7/10/12), the Treasury has over the past 30 years become dependent on a smaller and smaller proportion of tax-payers, with only the wealthiest 20 per cent paying significantly more to the state than they received in benefits and public services.

In 2011, 53.4 per cent of households received more in benefits and public services – such as health and education – than they paid in taxes. In 1979, the figure was 43.1 per cent. It had grown only to 43.8 per cent by 2001 and then accelerated as Labour's public spending boom, financed largely by borrowing, gathered pace.

In the first decade of the twenty first century, the number of households dependent on the state grew by 3 million, as a rise in benefits such as tax credits and spending on schools and hospitals took growing numbers of middle-income families into dependency on the state.

This reflects both increased spending by the government but also growing inequality with some people securing big rises in income while the less well-off had to make do on a much smaller rise.

Human beings have evolved to be ready to help each other so long as others are also ready to help them. If appeals for money to finance a social project are made, the evidence shows that the support is much stronger when people are actually aware that others have also given donations. The social security system however appears to involve our giving money through our taxes to be spent on people who don't themselves contribute.

d.) Effect on relations between the state and the individual

The state should be seen as representative and protector of us all. Sadly however, there is a state of conflict going on between the state which wants its payments to go only to those who need them and certain sections of the population who are suspected of taking more than their entitlement. Advertisements on TV and elsewhere are placed by the state to warn people of the consequences of dishonest claims for benefit.

e.) Damage to the quality of Britain's people

The overall effect of these weaknesses is a lowering of the character of the people. It is argued that people who are dependent on the state tend to be more easily led and less vigilant in defence of their freedoms than those who are not.

They are less likely to be responsible and self-reliant. The integrity of many has been undermined moreover and it seems so much easier to work for cash while still drawing benefit.

f.) Lack of choice

The ability of individuals to choose for themselves is widely regarded as the key element in a free society. People in Britain are free to choose where to buy what they want, work where they wish, consult with whomsoever they wish.

But for their own basic personal security they have no choice. They have to pay their national insurance contributions to the state and they have to depend on the state for their basic pension, for support in unemployment and for help in other emergencies. This emphasises their dependence on the state and is not consistent with our vision of the good society.

Adult citizens must be enabled to make their own arrangements to secure their financial independence. Having choice is a necessary condition for this.

9. *Concern that benefits misused*

Some taxpayers have felt that the money they pay to the government may be used to provide benefits to addicts who spend it on drugs and alcohol. In May 2012 Iain Duncan-Smith, Work and Pensions Secretary, warned that such people could be stripped of their benefits if they refused to accept treatment to tackle their addiction. In October 2012 it was reported (Sunday Times 14/10/12) that Iain Duncan-Smith had asked officials to examine an Australian system, which puts benefits on a "basics card", letting claimants buy food, clothing and fuel but not harmful items including drugs and alcohol. But this proposal raises a different concern: that the state will make payments only to those who behave in a way the government likes.

10. *The Beveridge Bequest*

What is remarkable, as pointed out by the Times (12/8/14) is that Beveridge, whose report laid the foundation for the Welfare State, was himself unhappy at this term and deeply troubled at the way the state was taking over what had been done by citizens and independent associations in the past.

Beveridge put his objections in a far less well-known follow-up to his original report in which he lamented the damage that state support was already doing to the capacity of individuals to help themselves.

11. Benefits for immigrants

In a proper system of insurance, benefits would be paid out just to those who had paid their contributions. But the British government soon abandoned that principle, took insurance payments as another form of income tax and paid out benefits to people irrespective of their contributions. Under this system, it was long accepted that benefits should be paid to immigrant workers who do not have their own income.

In the European Union citizens have the right to move to and work in other countries in the Union. Such moves were seen as a useful way of getting new skilled workers to operate in a new country of residence.

But the recession which began in 2008 led to a decline in employment and Britain's coalition government formed in 2010 was aware of the cost to social security of growing unemployment. The entry of workers from the EU could not be stopped but the government felt there must be a limit on the right of such workers to be paid benefits by the British government.

In September 2013, there were an estimated 100,000 EU immigrants in the UK. The EU was pressing that all such immigrants should receive benefits from the host country. Meanwhile, as reported by Brian Pancevski in the Sunday Times (20/10/13), there were some 10,000 British citizens in Germany claiming and getting unemployment benefit from the German government, even though 90 per cent had been judged fit to work.

These immigrants placed a high value on the fact that they were untroubled by the sort of "hassle" they face in Britain when the job centres tried to force them back to work. One complained that "patronising" officials in Britain had wanted him to take a job as a cleaner.

There were no such problems in Germany, where jobless Britons praised the ease with which they could make their claims and the regularity of the payments without further difficulties.

In 2013 the government became concerned that Romania and Bulgaria were joining the EU and that their citizens would have the right to work in Britain from January 2014. It decided that immigrants from these countries would not be able to claim benefits in their first three months in the UK.

On the 19th February 2014, the government announced that from April 2014, immigrants from the EU would not be able to claim certain benefits (including housing benefit) until they could prove that they had been working in Britain for at least three months and earning enough to pay national insurance (around £150 pw in 2014). This would entail working 24 hours a week at the minimum wage.

In the early summer of 2014, the Secretary of State Mr Duncan-Smith attacked what he termed "benefit tourism". People from Europe, he claimed, were coming to Britain to claim benefit.

"A good example of this is the Big Issue. What is happening progressively more and more is people mostly from southern and eastern Europe have ended up being Big Issue sellers and, as self employed, they claimed tax credits. So when we talk about benefits they are not just out-of-work benefits, they are also in-work benefits that are being claimed." The Big Issue accused Mr Duncan-Smith of trying to pass the buck for the loophole. "The flaws which he has highlighted were inherent in a benefits system created by the government and, to that extent, was the government's and not one of our making", a spokesman said.

The Big Issue was absolutely right. The benefit system is the creation of the government and if the system is used badly, there should be a different system.

The British government's attempt to cut benefits for immigrants from the EU also made some progress in the EU.

In November 2014 the European Court of Justice endorsed the decision by a German court that unemployment benefit could be denied to a Romanian woman in Leipzig who claimed it despite having no intention of working in Germany. Elizabeta Dano, 25, had never worked in Romania either, the court was told and turned down jobs offered by the Leipzig job centre. According to the court ruling: "A member state must...have the possibility of refusing to grant social benefits to economically inactive union citizens who exercise their right to freedom of movement solely in order to obtain another member state's social assistance, although they do not have sufficient resources to claim a right of residence."

Where the period of residence is between three months and five years – as it was in the German case – one of the conditions is that "economically inactive persons must have sufficient resources of their own."

In a potential boost to British attempts to restrict benefits to migrants, the ruling said that European Union rules on freedom of movement did not bar countries restricting certain payments, known as "special non-contributory cash benefits", to their own citizens. It made clear that national parliaments would have the right to determine who received this type of benefit and how much it was worth and the Charter of Fundamental Rights of the EU was therefore not applicable.

This judgement helped Britain's long-running fight against the commission over the legality of the "right to reside" test that Britain has used to restrict certain benefit payments unrelated to employment, including child benefit, child tax credit and jobseeker's allowance.

The judgement could also be used to impose extra restrictions on work related benefits.

By the end of 2014 (Times 21/1/15) the number of Britons claiming benefit in Germany was four times the number of Germans claiming benefit in the UK. The position with regard to Ireland was similar.

According to the Guardian (Times 21/1/15) there were, in 2014, 4 times as many unemployed Britons claiming benefit in Ireland as there were Irish doing so in the UK.

There were some 30,000 Britons claiming unemployment benefit in Europe. However there were 65,000 Europeans, mainly from the east, claiming benefit in Britain. There were some 14,880 Poles claiming jobseekers allowance for instance. Some Poles were also able to claim child benefit even if the children are still living in Poland with their mother. Such payouts are believed to cost Britain some £30m a year. This arrangement is enshrined in EU treaties so that Britain as a member could not just stop paying the benefit.

An assessment of the government's policy

The government maintains that immigrants to the UK have paid no tax in the UK and that it is unreasonable that British taxpayers should pay for benefits for these migrants. That is a perfectly valid point.

However it is also true that young British people seeking their first job have probably made no more financial contributions than the immigrants. So is it right that they should receive benefits while the immigrants do not?

In this case however it is up to the state to introduce a new system which enables all citizens both to contribute money to an institution which will then be able to pay out money to their contributors when they need it. How this can be done is explained in Part II. The state must also devise a scheme whereby immigrants can be covered for times in which they have no job.

12. Responsibility shared with local government

Another problem is that some of the money to be paid in benefits may have to be paid by local rather than central government. Central government should then reimburse local councils but it is not easy to get this right.

In December 2014 the government identified an amount for 2015/16 totalling £129.6mn nationally. On 4th February 2015 the government agreed to give local authorities an extra £74 mn for 2105/16 to cover social care as well as welfare.

In March 2015 the Local Government Association recommended that responsibility for the work programme for the unemployed should at least partly be passed to them.

In a report 'Realising Talent – A new framework for devolved employment and skills', published on 31st March 2015, the LGA set out proposals for government to devolve at least £15bn worth of employment and skills funding, arguing that councils and their partners were better placed to reduce long-term unemployment and can target support far better than the current national system. In particular, the LGA recommended the introduction of Local Labour Market Agreements across England by 2016/2017 to be the basis of a deal between groups of councils and central government on what is needed to get more people into work, help low paid people progress in work and address the skills demand for achieving local growth.

This is a sensible proposal. The work programme is almost the only part of the government's welfare policy that makes sense but it would be right to give local councils responsibility for it.

C. The coalition government's attempt to solve the problem – 2010-2015

It was not surprising that the coalition government in 2010 felt that the social security system should be radically reformed. Iain Duncan-Smith, Secretary of State for Work and Pensions set out his proposals in a white paper published in November 2010 and in due course most of these (with some amendment) passed through Parliament to come into effect in October 2013 – with a pilot scheme starting in April of that year.

The essence of the new system was that several different forms of benefit were to be combined in one Universal Credit to be paid monthly. Once fully implemented, Universal Credit should merge six existing benefits into one payment, covering some £70bn of benefit spending each year. It would also deliver savings of £35bn over a decade.

According to the Department of Work and Pensions (DWP) statistics published in July 2014, between April 2013 and 30th April 2014, 6960 people 'started' on Universal Credit'. Of these, the majority were male, with a male to female ratio of approximately seven to three and the majority of new claims were from unemployed people aged under 25. In addition, the statistics showed that on 30th April 2014 the total case load of Universal Credit claimants was 5,880 and that over six out of ten of those claimants were under the age of 25.

By October 2014 Universal Credit claims were being taken in around 50 Jobcentres and according to DWP statistics published on the 15th October 2014, 14,170 people were on the Universal Credit case load on 11th September 2014. At the same time, the DWP announced that universal credit would be available in all job centres from February 2015 to new single claimants previously eligible for Jobseekers' Allowance. In November 2014, DWP statistics showed that 17,850 people were on the universal credit case load as of October 2014.

The statistics also showed that of these 24 per cent were in employment and 59 per cent had been on universal credit for less than three months. Males aged 20-24 made up 27 per cent of the total case load. In February 2015 Iain Duncan-Smith stated that Universal Credit would be operating in every job centre across the country by February 2016 (Sunday Times 16/2/15).

Figures released by the DWP on 13th May 2015 showed that less than 100,000 people had so far made a claim for the new benefits and that on the 9th April 2015 there were just under 54,000 claimants on the universal credit case load, 16,740 in employment and 37,230 not in employment.

The government had originally imposed a cap of £26,000 on the total benefits provided to any household. In its manifesto for the 2015 General Election, the Conservative Party said it would lower this to £23,000 except for those receiving disability living allowance or the personal independence payment. The Conservative Party also planned to replace job seeker's allowance for 18 – 21 year olds with a youth allowance that would be limited to six months.

The government's main purpose was to reduce the costs of the benefit system and it is likely to be modestly successful in this. However its measures do not really help to remove the many weaknesses dealt with earlier. Moreover the efficiency measures have often made life harder for the claimants. One aspect of this was dealt with by the TUC in its report 'Universal Credit – the problem of delay in benefits payments' published in July 2014. This argued that one of the more controversial aspects of Universal Credit was the introduction in April 2015 of a new seven-day waiting period before an individual can claim benefit that will never be paid back. This was due to be introduced for Jobseeker's Allowance and Employment and Support Allowance in October 2014 and extend to Universal Credit in April 2015.

This report also pointed out that most claimants would face a long delay before they received their first payment. After claiming (and waiting seven days to become entitled), there would be a one calendar month (that is, usually about four and a half weeks) assessment of how much Universal Credit the claimant is entitled to. Following this, claimants have to wait a further seven days until payment is received, bringing the total waiting period to at least five weeks from the first day when the claim was made.

The reforms seem to be designed to make things harder for the claimant. The state is questioning appeals made and seems to be on the other side from where the claimant comes from.

A different system is needed, where the State withdraws and citizens are helped to be responsible and independent, able to make their own arrangements to deal with the money problems that arise.

D. Finding a better way

The preceding pages have shown that Britain's social security system just does not work; there is so much injustice, so much waste. There must be a better way.

1. Basic Income – A partial Solution

If our overwhelming concern is that everyone has sufficient means but that there is no means-testing, this can be achieved within a free society by the introduction of the Basic Income System. Every adult citizen would receive a basic income of £150 pw, say, from the state. Those who are able to work and choose to do so will pay tax on everything they earn and the revenue so raised will be used by the state to pay the basic income. The tax and benefits systems are integrated as one.

This, however, would cost the state's exchequer a great amount and taxes would have to be very high. If large numbers of people opted not to work, the burden on those who did would be excessive. Moreover, earning a living gives individuals a sense of purpose and achievement, while being able to 'get something for nothing' as a way of life turns an adult into a dependent child; it might also be resented by those providing the resources.

In 2015 however the Finnish government considered a pilot project under which each citizen would be given a fixed sum for a fixed period of time irrespective of whether they worked or not.

Before the General Election of 2015 the Green Party proposed a similar scheme. They argued that each citizen would receive £70 pw so that people could be given enough to tide them over if cut off from their expected income for a time.

2. *Charles Murray's proposal*

Charles Murray, in a book written in the United States but also in discussions with Civitas in the UK, proposed a variant of this basic income system. Under this scheme each adult would receive from the state the sum of say £8,000 pa to be paid in monthly instalments. There would be no other state support but the recipients would of course be able to work to increase their income.

They would also have to make a contribution of say £1,000 pa toward their pension and pay for their healthcare. Charitable institutions would have to help those citizens who were still unable to look after themselves.

This scheme, like the more generous Basic Income mentioned above, would certainly be better than the present system of means-tested benefits. But it has the same basic weaknesses. It makes people, at least partly, dependent on the state rather than free and responsible citizens in charge of their own lives.

3. *Policy Exchange proposal for compulsory unemployment insurance scheme*

In the autumn of 2014 the Policy Exchange think tank pointed toward a better way. Under the Policy Exchange proposals people working over 20 hours a week would contribute to a personal welfare account, amounting to at least £5 a week or £260 a year, offset by a reduction in national insurance contributions.

This would generate £8 bn a year of which £2 bn would go towards an unemployment insurance scheme partly to cover the costs of the first three months of unemployment, replacing the contributory element of jobseeker's allowance, whilst the remaining £6 bn would fund a system of individual welfare accounts.

The Policy Exchange also suggested that people would be able to top up their welfare accounts by up to £100 a week and that, in times of need, these accumulated savings should be used flexibly, for example, to fund retraining and, as such, would provide a greater level of support than jobseeker's allowance and universal credit.

Universal credit would act as a safety net for people who run down their pots or have a poor contribution record.

This scheme would not be administered by the government. Instead, to encourage providers to compete for customers based on their service and to ensure funds are sufficiently large to act as effective social insurance, a small number of providers (including insurer and fund managers) should be licensed to offer schemes to every individual. To limit exposure to uninsurable risks the government would guarantee the scheme as a lender of last resort, meaning that if unemployment rose significantly and unexpectedly government would cover the extra costs.

These proposals go some way towards a system in which all individuals are free and independent citizens, making their own arrangements, including insurance, to secure their future.

4. A principled approach

The right way to find an answer is to settle the principles which should govern the way in which society operates and then base the system of social security on those principles.

In part II, the nature of the principles and the way they should operate is examined and a system of social security which reflects those principles is put forward.

Part II

A Principled Approach to Welfare

1 Principles

How can services best be provided?

The way Britain's social security works, as shown in the first part of this book, should be a cause for shame. There are so many injustices and so much waste in the system that it must be changed. Before working out the answer it is necessary to go back to first principles and work out what is the best way for services to be provided. There are two models which have most been followed: the socialist model and the capitalist model.

A. The socialist model

1. The case for state control

It is tempting to believe that the most effective as well as the fairest way for services and products to be provided is for society to act collectively through the organs of the state. The state should have the capacity to work out what products are required by the members of society and could then plan to have these produced by state controlled enterprises, distributed and sold or at least provided by other organs of the state. In this way too everyone would have enough and no-one would consume too much: - the incomes of everyone would be controlled since all who worked would be the employees of the state.

This system of state control was practised longest and most completely by the Soviet Union from the 1920s until the 1980s. In the 1930's this system was in some ways more effective in preserving a basic standard of living with full employment than was the capitalist system practised in western countries

The way the British government, after June 1940, managed its resources to fight the Second World War strengthened the case for state control. It was the state moreover which provided the impetus for creating a better society after the war. An Education Act which provided for a better system was the result of investigations carried out by the government and it was passed through Parliament in 1944. It was the wartime government which appointed William Beveridge to come up with proposals for a better social security system and which accepted his report. After the war the Labour government created the National Health Service and brought other enterprises under state control. From 1945 until the 1980's Britain had a mixed economy with some services provided by the state and some by private enterprise.

2. The weaknesses of state control

From the 1960s to the 1980s however the total production of services and the material standard of living rose far more significantly in western free market economies than in the Soviet Union or the European members of the Socialist Bloc.

Where the state controls everything it can, moreover, make sure through the media that people are told what the government wants them to believe. This denies citizens that freedom and independence so beneficial to their moral and intellectual development and it deprives society of the benefits arising from the free exchange of ideas and so makes it harder to improve.

By the end of the 1980s the case for state socialism collapsed. It was increasingly felt that the most effective way of providing what people wanted was through distinctive enterprises competing with each other to provide the best possible product at the lowest available price. Individuals must be free to choose from which enterprise they obtain what they want at the price they deem acceptable.

If different enterprises compete this also gives people as workers greater freedom since they can give notice to one enterprise and take up employment at another requiring similar expertise. It also removes the collective power of the workers in an enterprise to force consumers to take the product it provides.

The weakness of state control became apparent in western democracies. In Britain during the 1980s Mrs Thatcher's government privatised various enterprises and this example was followed in many other countries. In the 21st century the government put the Post Office (Royal Mail) under private control in 2013.

However, the state in Britain is still the controller of many aspects of the country's activities and its wastefulness in carrying out its task is clear. The Times (02/02/09) published the results of its study, with Computer Weekly, of eight of the government's IT projects which showed that the overrun of the largest IT projects totalled £18.6 billion. Those included a controversial plan to computerise all NHS patient's records, originally estimated to cost £2.3 billion over three years but the cost of which had grown to £12.7 billion by 2009.

In 2008 QinetiQ, which had been working to provide the National Policing Improvement Agency with a system called Police Portal, sued the agency for £6.6 million after the project had been cancelled. QinetiQ's lawyers said that the agency had "failed to provide consistent and timely data" and was "routinely failing to return telephone calls or answer emails and correspondence." The claim was settled out of court and beyond the gaze of the public eye.

A former contractor, who worked with the Ministry of Justice on various computer projects in 2008 was quoted in The Times (03/02/09) as accusing the department of waste that "beggared belief". Speaking anonymously, the contractor said "Nothing is co-ordinated. You have about five or six separate companies all being paid millions to do not very much. And then a minister says something in Parliament and the whole project has to be changed." The contractor said that senior consultants for the department were paid up to £3,000 a day.

Ironically, some of the worst examples of the state's incapacity to spend money wisely comes from reports on foreign aid. According to a report by Jill Sherman in The Times (17.04.15) Britain is paying professional aid staff up to £1,000 a day to work in Africa and Asia as part of a spending "frenzy" to meet a government target.

Spending on consultants doubled in the past four years to £1.4 bn with the bill for outside help now eating up more than 10 per cent of the aid budget. The figures prompted anger among MP's who described the practice as a "grotesque waste".

"When people think of overseas aid they think of people who have had their homes damaged by an earthquake, a hurricane or a tsunami – they don't expect to be lining the pockets of consultant fat cats" said Philip Davies, the Tory parliamentary candidate for Shipley. "This is what happens when you are judged only by how much you are spending. How you actually spend the money becomes immaterial. It leads to grotesque waste and over-spending."

All three main political parties support Britain's legal commitment to devote 0.7 per cent of GDP to overseas aid. It has meant the budget soaring to £12 bn in two years and led to a rush to spend all the money.

An investigation by The Times found that hundreds of "team leaders" on aid projects earn at least £120,000 a year when accommodation, security, travel and expenses in poor countries are taken into account. Part-time daily rates of £800 to £1,000 are common. Consultancy firms are cashing in, with some benefiting from 50 per cent profit margins, according to insiders. Garth Glenworth, a former aid official in the government said that the Department for International Development (Dfid) relies on outside companies because it has too few staff. "It's a jolly lucrative business, believe me" said another former overseas aid official who is now a consultant. "Two areas did well out of the recession – development aid and pawnbrokers – both of whom are supposed to help the poor. Dfid's obese budget means it has to get the money out of the door as quickly as possible and the easiest way to achieve this is to have a few large programmes managed by a few suppliers. All of these features are going to contribute to a feeding frenzy among the consulting companies."

The total bill for consultants is likely to be significantly higher once spending on international agencies is taken into account. Half of the aid budget is sent directly to organisations such as the UN and the World Bank. Many of these agencies also employ outside advisers, meaning the total spend on consultants could be £3 bn or higher. Former civil servants also complained of a cosy group of 11 consultancy companies who win 60 per cent of the government's work. These include Adam Smith International, Atos, Coffey, Crown Agents and PwC.

The expenses of judge's lodgings has, as reported by Frances Gibb in the Times (17.6.15), caught the attention of Michael Gove, appointed Justice Secretary in 2015. The mansions, penthouses, flats and historic residences are used by the judiciary when at trials away from home. Michael Gove wants to look at the costs of the judges' lodgings to see if savings could be made to the annual £5 bn bill. Of the 32 lodgings, 16 cost the public purse more than £100,000 a year, including their chefs and housekeepers. Judges stay in them when travelling to crown courts outside London to hear the most serious criminal cases, such as murder. The lodgings stand empty for two thirds of the year. The most expensive of the residences is in Bristol, which cost the Ministry of Justice £552,442 in 2013-14, according to newly released figures. That works out at £46,000 a month or £10,600 a week.

In Leeds where the average house costs £170,000, judges are housed in a penthouse flat in Carr Manor, which costs £443,348 a year to provide. In Liverpool, where an average house costs £101,000 the annual cost is £426,634. Lodgings in Birmingham cost tax payers more, £406,366 and lodgings in Manchester cost £334,974. Tower House in Norwich comes complete with a butler's pantry and a folly in the grounds and costs £100,525 per year.

Ayers End house in Harpenden near St. Albans crown court costs £141,179 a year. The lodgings employ about 60 staff, such as house managers/butlers, chefs, housekeepers and cleaners. The Ministry spent a total of £4.87 million providing the lodgings in 2013-14, down from £5.12 million the previous year but up on the £4.56 million in 2011-12.

Where the state is responsible for enterprises whether schools, hospitals or roads, the funds it needs come mainly from taxation. But many people, although wanting more to be spent on important services, are understandably reluctant to pay more taxes: they see extravagance in government spending on advertisement, consultants, political advertising and computerisation projects that fail. It would be much healthier if people, insofar as they could, paid directly for the services they needed in a way consistent with social justice as well as free choice.

Of course wastefulness and fraud may occur in private enterprises as well as state ones. But an autonomous enterprise will collapse if income is insufficient to meet outgoings and it will have to take strict measures to avoid such unjustified leakage of money. If there is such waste in a state controlled enterprise the losses can be met by government funds obtained through taxation or borrowing. There is no automatic self-control. Expenditure is controlled from above.

Financial Transactions

The principle behind all financial transactions between individuals and independent bodies is that those who are buying a product or service bear the whole cost from their own resources while those who provide it receive whatever is paid and are able to add this to their own financial assets. Both parties must agree on the terms of the transaction before it takes place. Where the state is spending money, the integrity of financial transactions is undermined because the people acting on behalf of the state are not personally affected. A Minister, advised by a civil servant, agrees to spend £100,000 on a new computer system. The firm providing this receives £100,000 and adds this to its reserves. But neither the Minister nor the civil servant is personally affected. It is the state which pays.

But those responsible for the actions of the state are supposed to do so in the interests of society. They should feel like the parents of a young child who strive to do whatever is in the best interests of their offspring. William Gladstone probably thought in this way but many who now control public policy do not. The state's responsibility for financial transactions does not serve society well.

3. The provision of public services

If the state provides education in schools, as in the UK and most developed countries, it must first raise money by taxation which is politically controversial and subject to economic fluctuation. Then it employs civil servants to work out how much to give to each local council for all its purposes including education. Then the council decides how much to allocate to each school and finally each school is told what it has. How much simpler it is for an independent school to receive money direct from parents and then to spend it as it wishes!

Even bigger problems may arise in the distribution of funds for the healthcare service. Many thousands of people have been employed in passing money downwards. If a hospital starts to run out of money it may cancel operations until more cash is acquired at the start of the next financial year. The problem is that its income comes from above, not from those whom it serves. How much more sensible it would be if the patient could pay for his or her own treatment!

Ministers tend to favour keeping current spending low even if it leads to much higher expenditure later. Gordon Brown as Chancellor of the Exchequer used the Private Finance Initiative (PFI) to keep current expenditure on building a hospital low by giving the private firms building it the right to claim back large sums in future years from those then responsible for it.

State control also discourages responsibility. A responsible enterprise, like a responsible individual, can use a trading surplus to create reserves which can be drawn upon to meet possible future losses arising from an unexpected downturn in income or an increase in costs. But if an NHS Trust hospital has a surplus the state may take it away to cover losses in other hospitals. In March 2007 it was reported that the education department was planning to claw back funds from schools with a surplus. As it is, the government feels it has continually to check that public officials, schools and hospitals are spending their money well – so even more officials have to spend their time checking what's been done.

If Ministers feel responsible for enterprises such as hospitals and schools they will feel they must defend their work while political parties in opposition may use alleged inadequacies to attack the government so that vital services become political footballs. Such enterprises would benefit if the government ceased to be in control.

Where the state is responsible for enterprises whether schools, hospitals or roads, the funds it needs come mainly from taxation. But many people, although wanting more to be spent on important services, are understandably reluctant to pay more taxes: they see extravagance in government spending on advertisement, consultants, political advertising and computerisation projects that fail. It would be much healthier if people, insofar as they could, paid directly for the services they needed in a way consistent with social justice as well as free choice.

Of course wastefulness and fraud may occur in private enterprises as well as state ones. But an autonomous enterprise will collapse if income is insufficient to meet outgoings and it will have to take strict measures to avoid such unjustified leakage of money. If there is such waste in a state controlled enterprise the losses can be met by government funds obtained through taxation or borrowing. There is no automatic self-control. Expenditure is controlled from above.

4. The target culture

Since the nineties there has been an even more pernicious development. As Adam Curtis explained in The Trap on BBC2 in March 2007, governments have been persuaded that public servants are primarily in the job for their own gain. So it sets them targets and tells them that if they meet those targets they will get more money. Doctors and teachers who took on their work as a vocation now find themselves treated as fundamentally selfish people who can be motivated to teach better, to care for their patients better if they have the prospect of extra money dangled before them. It is hard for them to throw the money back; after all, they have mortgages to pay off, children to care for. So they meekly accept the money but with their self-respect undermined and no joy in their hearts.

As Simon Jenkins has commented (Sunday Times 25/03/07), a tradition of the public realm once built on autonomous institutions, elected leaders and public accountability has been overtaken by the demons of quantification and control. The means by which the Treasury regulates public money has become the means by which the centre controls everything on which money is spent.

To every activity is attached a pecuniary value and thus a performance. To every performance is attached a target and to every target a league table. The targets may seem to be guided by what people say they want in focus groups but in reality they are "negotiated" by power blocs within the public service. Their enforcement depends on matrices of budgets, feedback and incentives, covered by quasi-contracts and internal pricing systems.

Some see the answer as transferring control from central to local government. But interference from local controllers is in fact more harmful even than interference from central government! A local education controller is more likely to want to interfere.

Autonomous enterprises may well set targets for themselves and honestly seek to reach them. But targets imposed from outside are often resented.

5. Out sourcing

Government ministers are aware that work they manage themselves is likely to cost much more than would be the case if a private company undertook it. It is not surprising therefore that they ask such companies to undertake the work, usually after competitive tendering.

Having a public contract can be profitable but as Kiri Lolzan explained in an article in the Sunday Times (23/3/14) 'trying to win such a contract can be time consuming and costly for small companies'.

In 2013, £4.5bn of Whitehall's procurement budget went to small and medium-sized businesses. This amounted to only 10.5% of the external contracts awarded. "Small businesses can have their efforts to win public sector business hampered by excessive bureaucracy and bidding costs," said John Allen, Chairman of the Federation of Small Businesses.

The bidding process can mean days are sacrificed on a tender; time that could be spent on business. Some tender-writing companies charge thousands to pull together a bid and might want a cut of the business secured.

For those who have broken into the public sector, success has followed. One of them is Andy McLoughlin, 35, who runs Huddle, a software business that allows users to work and store information in the Internet cloud.

"Working with government provides an instant stamp of approval," said McLoughlin. But it wasn't easy. From the initial bid for the first state contract in 2008, it took three months to get a pilot of the service into government offices.

Whether the state does the work itself or pays a private firm to do it, the same basic weakness remains. The money spent does not belong to the people who spend it. It has been raised by taxation or borrowing and future generations have the job of paying interest on the money our generation has spent.

6. Is socialism dead?

In an article in the Times (13/6/15) Matthew Paris argued that socialism as an idea has been so widely discredited that, like the belief that the earth is flat, it should not be taken seriously. "This century's intellectual consensus should show Marxism the door. Whether strictly defined as public ownership of the means of production, distribution and exchange, or more loosely as state direction of the 'commanding heights' of the economy, socialism must be counted as definitively discredited. Over almost a century that theory has been tested – in every case – to destruction. To bring the public understanding up to date with this is overdue". Matthew Paris goes on to make the case for capitalism – but that's another story.

B. The capitalist model

1. The case for capitalist control

In modern western capitalist economies large enterprises may be owned by mainly absent shareholders who provide the capital while the managers are regarded as agents expected to secure the best dividends and capital growth for the shareholder. The workers have traditionally been represented by trade unions. Many of the weaknesses of state control are removed in the capitalist model. Under state control, the funds come from above. Under capitalist control, as in other privately owned enterprises, the money comes from those who want the product.

The customer will almost always have a choice since the service is provided not by one enterprise but by several competing ones each seeking to provide what people need. This competition should keep the price and cost of production as low as the enterprise can reasonably make it. Enterprises moreover are ready to take risks and to undertake research to find new products.

2. The weaknesses of capitalism

The system has however many intrinsic weaknesses.

First there is the potential conflict between managers responsible to shareholders and the people who work in the enterprise. This conflict may occasionally erupt into 'industrial action' by workers demanding better pay or conditions. The basic inequity of the structure is also seen occasionally in the apparently sudden decision of a company to close down a factory or other place of work and thus to terminate the employment of those who work there. In such cases workers are entitled to statutory redundancy payment but this does not alter the impression conveyed that people are merely tools in the operation of a business to be discarded if necessary.

Another weakness in a system of ownership by absentee shareholders is that shares can be purchased by another enterprise, perhaps based in another country. Many of the utilities privatised in the 1980's, such as water supply and electricity, have been taken over by firms in France or Germany. It could be dangerous to have such vital services not owned by those based in this country. France does indeed seek to protect such enterprises from foreign ownership.

As Will Hutton pointed out in his programme 'Selling off Britain' on Channel 4 (21/3/15) a large part of the water industry is owned by foreign firms. Thames Water is an example of a privatised public service becoming foreign controlled. A study of their accounts showed that they were not using profits to provide for future development. Profits have been used to boost the payments to shareholders while money has been borrowed to fund future development.

Many British firms have come under foreign ownership because shareholders have sold their shares to bidders from foreign countries. Cadbury was for many years run by a family which devoted much of its profit to improving the lives of their workers, even building houses for them. After 1969 the company sold shares to raise money and eventually lost control. In 2010 the American company Kraft intervened to buy shares to get control. British financial operators bought Cadbury shares in the hope of making a good profit by selling them to Craft, which was then able to take over the company.

Earlier another great and well established company, ICI, came under foreign control in 2008 when it was taken over by a Dutch firm and dismembered. Even our television companies are open to foreign control. Channel 5 is now in American ownership.

Will Hutton was rightly concerned at the large-scale sale of British businesses into foreign ownership to the tune of £440 bn between 2004 and 2014. He has argued that this trend may lead to a dumbed-down low wage low productivity Britain in which we lose control of almost any industry where we still have high standards.

This 'dumbing-down' of what are perfectly valid and operationally efficient methods – leading to high standards – is reflected in computing world wide. Apple Inc (15th largest company in the world by revenue and 2nd by market capitalisation), Microsoft (3rd largest by market cap) and Google (4th by market cap) are increasingly offering apparently simple ways of doing things, yet the systems unseen by the people that use them create greater co-ordinated control than ever before. This would be seen as a great issue but for the powerful, all-pervasive computer systems now spanning the earth.

A problem may also arise if a firm operating in the UK but based overseas chooses in times of economic downturn to employ people from its own country in preference to UK nationals. But it is the underlying philosophy of the capitalist model – that its main job is to make money – that is most damaging both to those who work in the enterprise and those to whom it proffers its services.

The staff are encouraged to want to make money for themselves as well as for the company. Often bonuses are awarded for the amount of business they generate – so the need to sell a product becomes more important than to provide what is best for the purchaser.

People of quality, so long as their basic needs are met, know that their capacity to live a good and effective life depends primarily not on their financial assets and material possessions but rather on their intellectual capacity and character. But people of lower quality may be driven by a firm's bonus culture to put their own financial gain first to the detriment not only of those they are supposed to serve but also, as in the banks, of the firm itself. Commercial enterprises may also do harm to the values of individual lives as well as of society.

The success of such enterprises depends upon the level of sales of their products or services being at least maintained and at best advanced so that the earnings of workers and returns to capital providers can be steady at least and at best increased. To secure the expansion of sales, enterprises advertise their wares so that individuals may be persuaded to buy more and more, even if they have no pressing need to do so. So more and more clothes, appliances and other material objects are thrown away before their time thus creating more and more waste with great potential damage to the environment and more and more production of more goods.

People think they need more and more money to spend on these goods and they borrow more and more to pay for them. People become therefore more concerned with the material quality of their lives rather than with the far more important intellectual and moral quality. Individual lives are damaged as well as the environment.

The way in which society works has been deeply affected by the operation of the capitalist model.

If enterprises are to be able to provide profit for their owners and good wages for their staff they must sell more so more and more people must be persuaded to buy their products. So there is extensive advertising, both on television and in the press as well as in many other ways. But people will only be able to buy the goods if they have money. So customers are told that if they want to buy a product costing £1000 they can do so by making 12 or so monthly payments of £100. They can take the product and pay later. So consumers owe large sums to the providers of the money which they need to borrow.

In the middle of the 20th century many thinking people hoped and expected that as productivity improved people would not need to work so much. They could spend more time with the family or in furthering their education. It would certainly continue to be the case that the parents at least would always be at home during the early years of childhood. Sadly this has not happened.

The success of the capitalist model depends upon selling more and more and people must be fully employed in making more money.

The media and the government seems to think that what matters most is economic growth. If the economy can grow by 2% per annum then everything is seen to be fine. Instead of being able to live a good and fulfilling life, people are urged to make more money and own more things.

Giles Fraser, in his 'thought for the day' on Radio 4 (1/1/15) commented on the significance of the Marshmallow Test. Young children were asked whether they would like to have one marshmallow now or two in twenty minutes. Those children who chose to wait to get two later were found to live more successful lives in the future.

Those European countries who adopted the Protestant ethic with its encouragement of saving in the future were better able to develop their economic resources.

Western countries in the twenty first century are failing the Marshmallow Test. People are encouraged not to save for the future but to borrow money so they can buy now and pay later.

In an article in the Guardian (22/6/15) Giles Frazer commented on an extremely significant weakness of capitalism. It does not make a moral distinction between what people want and what people actually need between say Playstations and penicillin. It produces what people want not what they really need. If the market demands rubbish, capitalist controlled firms will produce rubbish meeting short term wants rather than long-term needs. Whatever firms produce, what matters in the capitalist system is growth, producing more things that people want, not what society needs.

Can the capitalist model be amended in a way which will remove these weaknesses? Will Hutton may think so. As Peter Wilby reminded us in his article in The Guardian (21/2/15), his book 'The State We're In' published in January 1995 and his concept of "stakeholder capitalism" offered an alternative to the profit-driven, short-termist free market that had developed in Britain during the 1980's. Companies' decisions, Hutton argued, should have regard not only to their shareholders' interests but also to those of their employees, suppliers and consumers and indeed to the interests of the nation and the planet. That would give Britain higher and more consistent economic growth as well as a more equal and cohesive society. Stakeholder capitalism, some thought, was the "big idea" that was needed.

In 2015, Will Hutton again put forward his views in a new book 'How Good Can We be?' But this book, like his earlier one failed to deal with the fundamental weakness of capitalism: that large enterprises are owned by shareholders whose primary aim is usually not the good of others but their own pecuniary gain.

The best way to live is to help others. If people seek first their own material good then, whatever the consequences the aim of the capitalist enterprise is inconsistent with living the good life.

As Matthew Paris wrote in his Times article (13/6/15) "You cannot have a successful modern democracy without free-market economics. You cannot have free-market economics without the profit motive. You cannot have the profit motive without letting the pursuit of private profit weave itself intimately into the fabric of ordinary citizen's lives. Until we face this, until we learn it morally as well as intellectually, we skew not only our politics but our habits of thought. Why is Adam Smith not held out to schoolchildren as Charles Darwin is: as a scientist who's analysis is now the consensus among most thinking people? Why is elementary market economics not taught routinely to schoolchildren?"

Matthew Paris accepts capitalism; letting the pursuit of private profit weave itself intimately into the fabric of ordinary citizens' lives. But the pursuit of private profit has no place in nobler visions of humanity.

3a) *The banking crisis 2007-09 and the subsequent economic breakdown*

Events leading to the banking crisis of 2007-09 illustrate the fundamental weakness of the capitalist model.

Retail banks like building societies had traditionally paid interest to those who saved and then charged higher interest on those who borrowed from them, keeping capital in reserve to deal with situations in which their balance would otherwise be in the red. If a bank lent money to somebody to buy a house the buyer would personally be responsible to it for paying back the loan with interest. The bank was technically the owner of the house until the borrower had completed making the payments due under the mortgage arrangement.

In the early twenty-first century banks adopted a new system in order to make money: securitisation. They put together a number of loan agreements (under which they were due to receive a monthly income) in a bundle and sold it off as a distinct security: a Collateral Debt Obligation (CDO). The finance houses and other City banks were happy to pay a good price for these CDO's which gave them a good regular income. With the money thus obtained the lending banks were able to offer more loans, often without sufficient concern for the borrower's ability to pay the mortgage due.

So instead of depending on savers to provide their income these banks increasingly depended on other financial institutions buying their loan stock from them in the form of CDO's. Meanwhile they used the money they were getting from these transactions to lend more and more to those seeking to buy a property.

In the past banks had expected a long-term relationship with their borrowers and had been careful to lend to people with the capacity to repay what they had borrowed. Now they expected to sell on these loans in a bundle (the CDO) to other financial institutions. So the borrower's capacity to repay was not vital to them. Staff were paid bonuses on the amounts of business they generated.

So banks, particularly in the USA and Britain, increasingly lent money to house owners who did not really have the long-term capacity to repay the loan: sub-prime mortgages.

Some staff, concerned only to make business, would even encourage potential buyers to certify that their homes were worth more than was really the case. The result was that the cost of houses rose steeply, taking them out of reach of the less affluent but also saddling many new home owners with debt obligations they would not be able to meet.

Those who worked in the banks, thanks to the extent of the business they acquired, received increasing pay and bonuses. But the direct relationship between bank and individual borrower had been broken.

The crash had to come. In Britain the first casualty was Northern Rock. This had been established in the middle of the nineteenth century as a building society serving, in particular, the north-east of England. It was of course a mutual society, owned by its members: the majority who saved with the society and the others who borrowed from it to buy a house. It played an active part in supporting community life and was widely respected. Then in the late 1990's, it persuaded its members to vote to become a bank in which they were initial shareholders. Shares were then sold to others who wanted to invest in the bank for financial gain.

Northern Rock's main aim now was to make more money both for its shareholders and its staff. It soon found it could do this by selling on bundles of loans as CDO's to other financial institutions and then using the money to make more loans, often unwisely, for the purchase of property.

Eventually however these financial institutions, on whom the bank relied to buy its loan stock, began to realise the possible dangers of having loan stock in sub-prime mortgages and no longer provided Northern Rock with a market.

It soon no longer had the income to pay its savers and staff and meet its other obligations. In the late summer of 2007 it applied to the Bank of England for a loan. This was publicised and savers with the bank started to queue outside its branches in large numbers to withdraw their savings. The bank was broken: the government then had to take control, guarantee savers their money and eventually nationalise it. But the crisis was far bigger than Northern Rock. The big banks had been buying these bundles of loans (CDO's) from each other as well as from others. They now realised that many of the loans might be worthless. They were no longer prepared to buy them. In the summer and autumn of 2008 banks became unwilling to lend to each other.

By the autumn of 2008 it became clear that many banks had huge debts and would be unable to carry on. In Britain the government had to take Bradford and Bingley into state control and put £20bn into the Royal Bank of Scotland to give it a 60% share of the equity and put £11.5 bn into HBOS which had to merge with Lloyds TSB to keep going. On 3rd February 2009 the Bank of England revealed that it had lent £185bn to banks in the last few months. It has been subsequently accepted that without government action the banking system would have collapsed.

As it was the banks, saddled with debt as they were, were naturally very cautious about lending to businesses, some of which, without credit, collapsed or reduced their operations, laying off staff. Four and a half thousand businesses in the UK went into liquidation in the last quarter of 2008, 50% more than in 2007.

Thanks to the failure of the banks, Britain as well as the USA and other developed countries moved into a recession which brought hard times for many ordinary people. This crisis shows clearly that the capitalist model for banks and other financial institutions has failed and needs to be replaced.

3b) The continued misbehaviour of bankers

In spite of the mess they had created in 2008-9, when some banks were on the edge of collapse, bankers continued to use clients as a means to making money for themselves.

They were found to have sold Payment Protection Insurance (PPI) to their clients although it was not in their interest. Banks have had to pay millions of pounds to those they misled.

Their misuse of foreign exchange markets was only known in 2012. Foreign exchange traders were paid to arrange currency exchange helpful to their clients. Instead, the traders and others would congregate in chat rooms an hour or so before benchmark rates were set to discuss their aggregate trading positions and how to execute them to their mutual benefit. They manipulated the WM/Reuters currency benchmark, which is used to determine the value of index tracker funds around the world. The rate, known as the fix, is set for more than 130 currencies by taking a snapshot of trades in the 30 seconds before and after 4 pm. in London.

If the traders all had orders in the same direction, they would seek to turbocharge any price moves. In the minutes before the fix, they would attempt to sniff out any banks with large orders in the other direction and trade with them in advance, a process known in the market as 'taking out the filth'. At other times they would trade with third parties outside the chat room with the intention of giving them orders in the same direction to execute at the fix.

"The traders put their own interests ahead of their customers, they manipulated the market – or attempted to manipulate the market – and abused the trust of the public", FCA CEO Martin Wheatley told reporters at a briefing in London without identifying which traders he was talking about. The regulator would press firms to review their bonus plans and claw back payments already made.

The fines were the largest the British regulator had imposed and mark the first time it has entered into a group bank settlement.

At the annual inclusive capitalist event in June 2015, Mark Carney, Governor of the Bank of England expressed his concern not only about the behaviour of the banks but also the non-bank financial sector, involving private equity and hedge funds. According to the Times (27/6/15) Mr Carney said "You cannot have an industry that big unless it has social license and acceptance"

The bank has taken decisive action to clamp down on bad behaviour in the wake of the flood of scandals in the City, including foreign exchange and Libor rigging. However, he added that some bankers still did not know how to behave. "A lot of people in this market didn't know and probably still don't know, what is expected of them. There is no case history, no examples to follow" he said. The bank's answer has been a sweeping reform programme, including plans to make senior managers far more responsible for the management of their institutions under the forth-coming senior managers regime. But is it possible for privately owned capitalist enterprises to put the country and their clients first?

Marx's view on capitalism

In the late nineteenth century Marx's critical analysis of capitalism, Das Kapital, as quoted by Jennifer Hill in the Sunday Times (01/02/09), had warned that "owners of capital will stimulate the working class to buy more and more expensive goods, houses and technology, pushing them to take more and more expensive credits, until their debt becomes unbearable. The unpaid debt will lead to bankruptcy of banks, which will have to be nationalised and the state will have to take the road which will eventually lead to communism".

As shown earlier in this chapter, however, state control of enterprise does not work well and has damaging effects. There has to be a better alternative.

C.   Finding a new model.

What are the qualities needed by an enterprise providing services for people? What is the good enterprise?

1. *Prime purpose must be to serve others*

Just as an individual to live the best life must care for the interests of others, so must an enterprise accept the overriding imperative to look after the interest of those it is supposed to serve. Of course the enterprise must be concerned with the interest of those who work in or manage it and with those who provide the capital – but 'the customer comes first!' whether children at school or shoppers in the supermarket. Just as cars and human beings are evaluated according to their capacity for being of use to other individuals or society, so must an enterprise be evaluated on its capacity for the service of others.

There is an alternative view: that the purpose of an enterprise (other than if it is owned by the state) is to serve the owner's good, primarily through the acquisition of money. The owner may be an individual, partners, a group of individuals or shareholders but in all cases the object is to increase their financial assets.

Adam Smith famously pointed out that if an enterprise, a shop or a factory, say, aims to increase the income of the owners then, so long as there is competition, it will seek to sell or produce the best possible goods at the lowest possible price consistent with the profitability of the business. By seeking their own profit, the owners of the enterprises do what is best for their customers.

The contrary is equally true. If the owners of enterprises put their customers first and seek to provide them with the best possible goods at the lowest possible price consistent with the profitability of the business (on which future ability to provide the goods depends), then the customers will buy from them and this also leads to their own financial gain. What is good for the customers may well be the same as what is good for the enterprise itself. If ever, however, the owners of the enterprise put their own personal financial profit ahead of the good of the customer then they are behaving in a way which is inconsistent with what should be their purpose as individuals. Some of the ways this may be done have been identified in the previous section outlining the weaknesses of the capitalist system.

2. Income must come from those served

An enterprise should derive its income from those it serves. In this way those benefiting from the service know what they have paid for. If income comes from above, as with state-owned enterprises, there is no easy way of knowing how well the money has been spent. The state has to spend time and money checking how well the service has been delivered.

3. Financial viability

The enterprise is unlikely to be successful in meeting its purpose unless it is financially viable. As with the individual, income must in the medium term be sufficient to meet expenditure if the enterprise is to survive. A surplus income over expenditure (profit) is necessary to attract investment. But profit is good whatever the enterprise – because even after obligations are met the balance provides reserves for future development. Profit also provides the means to raise levels of remuneration for the staff or to lower price to the customer.

Efficiency is a constant goal in any successful enterprise since it is the key to providing better products, whether services or physical goods, at lower cost or effort.

4. *Working together: commitment, cohesion and communication*

Clearly an enterprise is more likely to be successful if all involved in it work together and feel a sense of common purpose. The *commitment* to the enterprise of all its members is important to its success. As an enterprise expands there will be a danger that individuals become less committed because they no longer believe that they they themselves are important to it.

Cohesion, or solidarity, is important for a good and successful enterprise as it is for a good society. Those who devote their working lives to the enterprise must all feel a part of it, sharing responsibility and rewards. Without such cohesion, where workers and managers regard each other as enemies, the enterprise does not deserve to survive. Pay rates must vary according to the level of ability and responsibility but not be so different as to engender dissatisfaction in the lower paid. This sense of cohesion is strengthened if ownership is shared by all who work in the enterprise, as at John Lewis.

Good *communication* between all is important to securing the commitment and cohesion of employees.

The importance of good communications is the central theme of A Little More Conversation, a report by the workplace communications consultancy CHA published in October 2005 based on interviews with 1,000 employees across Britain and carried out with Astra Zeneca's help.

The central theme that emerged from this study was how good communications could transform corporate performance. Steve Newall, UK managing director of DDI, a global HR consultancy that contributed to the survey, argues that people need to see meaning in their work: "Where we see high levels of employee commitment, it's because managers take trouble to share the big picture with their people and help them recognise their part in it."

David Prager, a communications leader at Astra Zeneca, has no doubts about the importance of good corporate communication. Getting it right is essential if employees are to boost the group's fortunes. "The engagement of the staff is absolutely critical to our success", he said. "Their motivation is increased when they understand the company's objectives. There is a clear link between what the company is trying to do and their role. What is particularly important is that these individuals understand the meaning of that success".

5. Devolution

A large enterprise may be able to operate more effectively if it is subdivided into largely autonomous sections where the control, except in very major issues, is based. However there will be other functions which can be taken so much more efficiently at the centre. A supermarket chain, for instance, will take buying and pricing decisions at the centre while leaving a manager in charge of operations at a particular supermarket.

If however managers feel that they have little power in making big decisions, their commitment to the enterprise may reduce. This seems to have happened at Sainsburys before the appointment of Justine King as Chief Executive. According to "Meaning Inc: The Blueprint for Business Success in the 21st Century" written by Gurnek Bains et al and published by Profile Books in 2006 "by the time Justine King had arrived, store managers were being assessed and monitored on a plethora of different measures to the extent that they felt they couldn't move without contravening some control or other that had been placed on them." King quickly moved to make changes at head office and give power back to the stores. His moves had a palpable impact on the promotion of managers and their sense of accountability and responsibility of what happened on their next watch. It also proved a long over-due turning point, with Sainsbury's supermarket share rising for the first time in years.

6. *Integrity*

Integrity is as vital to the quality of the enterprise as it is to a human being. First, the enterprise itself must keep careful accounts of all payments and receipts, including VAT and ensure that it provides an accurate statement of income on which tax is to be paid.

It might help if accountants carrying out an annual audit were appointed and paid not, as now, by the enterprise itself but by an independent authority appointed by the government (which could get some of its costs back by a charge on each enterprise for the services provided). If one business fails to pay the proper tax this can enable it to undercut the honest traders who are then themselves tempted to be dishonest.

7. *Autonomy*

The enterprise must, like an individual, be autonomous, as free as possible from outside control subject to the requirements, such as justice and cohesion, of the good society. The autonomous enterprise is in charge of its own finances, makes its own appointments, monitors its own performance in providing goods and services.

8. *Competition & choice*

In order to do their best, many people need the spur of competition. If others are working to provide the same goods or service then an enterprise cannot afford not to be efficient. There must be a market which enables consumers to decide which enterprise provides the service or goods which best meet their needs.

D.   The Third Way: the Autonomous Trust

In the last section the qualities needed by a good enterprise were set out. The socialist model and the capitalist model both fail for different reasons. We have to find a third way. This could be the Autonomous Trust which should take over responsibilities for most enterprises which are currently run by the state as well as of those which are currently owned by shareholders.

Schools and hospitals for instance should become autonomous trusts, securing their revenue not from above but from below, from those who benefit from their services or those who act for them, from patients and parents, for instance. Such autonomous enterprises should compete to provide the best possible service. Apart from a nationally established inspection service government can keep out.

A good model is provided by the independent presently fee-paying 'public schools'.

The Board of Trustees or Governors should manage each educational and healthcare enterprise without any external interference although the operation of the enterprise should be subject to inspection. But their income must come from payments made by or on behalf of those they serve.

Although the school or hospital must be run as an autonomous trust, the buildings used could be rented from either a commercial company or an organ of government with terms and costs agreed in advance by the two parties.

There must moreover be limitations on its freedom.

1. *Fair access*

If a system of competing enterprises is left to itself it may develop symptoms which do not accord with the qualities of the good society. Equality of opportunity is a necessary aspect of the principle of justice. All children irrespective of their home should as far as possible have the same chance to develop physically, intellectually and morally.

The chance children have of a good education must not therefore depend for instance on the income of their parents, nor on their race or religion.

Equality of esteem and equality of citizenship rights are also necessary in a just society. This means for instance that all citizens, whatever their income, should have the same opportunity for good healthcare when it is needed. Hospitals must compete with each other in offering the best service and patients or those acting for them must be free to choose. But the principle of 'equality of esteem' dictates that each potential patient has the same capacity to pay for the service.

Management of the market for education and healthcare is necessary however not only for the sake of justice but also to ensure that all individuals can become their best selves. The character of someone who would otherwise put intellectual and moral quality ahead of material gain is undermined if the only way to get good healthcare and a good education for the children is by having to earn enough to pay for it. Where possible people are best served where they have access to competing providers so long as the principles of justice operate and the character of individuals is not undermined. Each person must be in a position to pay the same sum for the service required.

2. Freedom of choice

An individual must be able to exercise freedom of choice insofar as this does not harm others.

A child must not be allocated to a school by public authorities: the parents must be free to choose. Some method must be found to ensure that schools compete for pupils while parents choosing the school all have the same capacity to pay for the education provided. Where there are more applications to attend a school than places available then there must be a generally agreed procedure for determining the fairest way to identify the children who can be accepted. Brothers or sisters of children already at the school should of course be admitted. Otherwise children living in specified areas could be given priority.

Similarly, citizens, perhaps through their agent, should be able to choose which hospitals they attend and in which GP surgery they enrol while at the same time being able to pay for whatever they choose. The two principles of equality of opportunity and freedom of choice must apply.

The way in which this situation can be created must now be explained.

3. Method of operation

It has been argued in section (2) above that enterprises, like individuals, thrive best if they are as free as possible so long as this is within the constraint necessary to be consistent with the principles of the good society. To be autonomous an enterprise must secure its income from those who use its services: this can be done for schools, colleges, hospitals and primary healthcare by means of the part-paid for, full-cover voucher as explained below. The enterprise controls this income and decides on its policy and development.

Those who work in these institutions have done so for the most part out of vocation. Young people have chosen to be teachers or doctors as a way of serving the community. This sense of vocation may have been eroded in recent years as the importance of money has been magnified but if such people are to be helped to be their best selves this possible decline should be reversed. Were teachers for instance to work for a private profit-seeking company, this vocation would be further undermined. The teacher and doctor work to help their pupils and patients: if the success of their work brings profit to shareholders or even more money for themselves that is to miss the point of the whole operation. The school, college or hospital must be owned by an Autonomous Trust which exists to serve those who need what it offers.

4a) An example – hospitals

The hospital is an example of a publicly provided institution becoming an Autonomous Trust.

Hospitals could be self-financing enterprises run as Trusts, meeting all the costs including those related to the premises, such as rent as well as paying all salaries. They will secure their income from those people who use their services and to whom they are accountable.

Everyone must be insured to meet the cost of hospital treatment when it arises.

There must be universal insurance, allowing everyone to choose and pay. There should be no charges at the point of use and people should have freedom to choose between competing providers of healthcare insurance. There must be an effective and fair means of payment which is consistent with the principle of justice, that all citizens have the same right to good healthcare.

The state has to ensure that individuals have the ability to pay for treatment at whichever hospital they choose, irrespective of their income or place of abode. It can secure this by issuing all citizens with a Health Insurance Voucher (with its value depending on their age). It must also ensure that there are at least 3 or 4 health insurance societies which will then be required (i) to accept the insurance voucher from any citizen as sufficient payment and (ii) to pay a hospital for services it has provided for one of its members on terms within nationally agreed guidelines. Everyone will pay for this voucher (the cost depending on their age) to the extent that their income allows.

Let us say, for ease of our calculations, that the value of a voucher for a single man in his late thirties is fixed at £700 p.a., the tax rate is 20%, the single person's allowance is £12,500 and the man's income is £35,000 p.a. He first pays £100, say, for his local health centre registration voucher as 20% of his first £500 of reserved (taxable) income i.e. above £12,500. Then he pays £400 for the Health Insurance Voucher as 20% of the next £2,000 of his income, so that 20% of the £2,500 of his income above £12,500 is used to acquire healthcare vouchers. His new 'second threshold' for the purpose either of tax or other levies is now £12,500 + £2,500 i.e. £15,000. The allowance (£12,500) may be raised to take account of Life Fund payments as explained in the next part of this text.

If the total income of the single person was less than £12,500, then the Health Finance Agency (HFA) would provide the Health Insurance Vouchers without charge and would recoup by a payment from the government. Most older people would need vouchers of higher value.

Those earning enough to pay for the vouchers in full would, if they so wish, arrange to pay the sum due direct to their health insurance society by direct debit from their bank, simply giving a copy of the agreement to HMRC and their employer who would not then need to make any deduction for this purpose and who would so inform the HFA. Alternatively such an individual would be able to ask their employer to pay the sum due direct to the insurance society.

All payments, income and expenditure, will be made through, by or in consultation with the HFA. All the government has to do is to pay whatever is necessary to ensure that the less well-off people are able to have a voucher for full health cover.

4b) Another example – banks

Banks are capitalist enterprises which most clearly should become autonomous trusts.

Financial institutions dealing with ordinary people who wish to save, borrow, buy a house or insure their lives or property should be autonomous trusts always putting first the interests of the individual being advised but still of course needing to make money to cover all their costs and to make a profit for future development. Building societies are already autonomous trusts of this nature. Banks lending to individuals must be motivated by a similar sense of responsibility: not lending to customers whose ability to repay the loan is suspect, not touting for borrowers or paying commission to those who enrol them.

For this development to take place, retail banks must first be divided from investment banking. Shareholders will become stockholders; the value of their investment will be assessed and this sum will belong to them and be converted into loan stock. The bank will be run as a business paying interest on the money invested in it. Some loan stock could have interest relating directly to the profit made by the business. Other loan stock would offer a fixed rate of interest for a specific number of years. The former shareholder must decide in which way he would invest his money.

But the prime purpose of each retail bank must be to offer the best possible service to those who use it. The former shareholders now stock holders will have no direct influence on the policy of the bank or on the composition of its leadership.

5. *What about Social Security?*

Society will partly be assessed by the degree to which all its members have sufficient means to live as satisfactorily as their physical condition allows. The state therefore must ensure that everyone has the means to secure what is needed for basic living costs. To do this the state now runs a huge and costly welfare system which has been described in Part 1.

Millions of pounds are lost through inefficiency and fraud. Injustices abound, particularly in means-tested benefits, for which people only qualify if their income is below a certain point so that saving is discouraged and cheating (by not declaring income in full) becomes too easy and too tempting.

What now has to be done is to see how the social security system can be released from the incompetent hands of the state and re-modelled on the principles set out above.

Part II

A Principled Approach to Welfare

2 Proposals

A. Principles

You don't really solve big problems in established structures by trying to solve them. A pragmatic approach to a particular problem may lead to improvement but from time to time it is necessary to scrap an existing structure and build a new one based on how we think things should be in the best possible society.

In the UK, the Welfare State system needs such an upheaval now. Of course all our citizens individually or in families must have an income sufficient to meet the cost of basic needs not only in normal times but also in difficult times, when ill or unemployed, when involved in full-time education and in old age.

But 'man does not live by bread alone'. The quality of life depends not only upon material circumstances but also upon its intellectual and moral quality. To be their best selves people need to be free, responsible and independent.

The state must not undermine but should rather help people to be their best selves in non-physical as well as physical terms. People need to have enough money for daily living but they should also develop the qualities of intellect and character necessary for them to be responsible independent citizens free to manage their affairs in the way they choose, so long, of course, as they do not damage others or society as a whole.

The quality of society also matters. We should aspire to build a just society, giving its citizens equality of opportunity, a cohesive society, of which everyone feels a member, an honest society supported by the integrity of its citizens, a free society, giving its members freedom of choice and an efficient society, able to secure the end it seeks.

The quality of our lives depends also on the intermediate associations in society, in particular the nature of the enterprises which provide us with the goods and services we need. Such enterprises as shown in the previous chapter are most effective as autonomous trusts competing to provide the best service.

A social security system then should ensure that its citizens enjoy sufficient material circumstances but must do so in a way which is consistent with the enhancement of their intellectual and moral quality. It must operate not under the control of a bureaucratic state but through the work of autonomous intermediate enterprises whose purpose is to serve those who come to them and who compete on a level playing field.

As David Green put it in his pamphlet "An end to welfare rights" published by the IEA in 1999 (p.67): "People who wish to be free and responsible members of a community require a lifetime plan of action to allow them to be self-sufficient and thus also to make a positive contribution to the wealth and well-being of society". They have to be able to look ahead with confidence and understand the financial parameters within which they live. As David Green also commented in the pamphlet (p.68): "One of the chief defects of many welfare benefits is that paying them can reduce work effort". This damage to work effort undermines self-reliance and thus actively makes it harder to get out of poverty. The whole social security system that we have inherited must be scrapped and a new one based on these principles must be introduced to replace the old. How such a system might work is explained in the next section.

B   The Life Fund

1. How the system would work

(a) Payments

The existing system of National Insurance and social security benefits must be replaced. Instead a Life Fund must be established into which all citizens pay contributions through most of their working life and from which payments can be taken (a) to meet the expected – or at least not entirely unexpected – demands of life: short term unemployment, temporary inability to work through illness or injury, being involved in adult education full or part-time, having children and (b) for the years of old age.

For a given number of years (say, 40 years) individuals will contribute to their Life Fund a weekly fixed sum (say, £40) for 50 of the 52 weeks of the year (£2,000 pa). This sum will be deducted at source for employed persons (in the same way as National Insurance contributions have been collected) and passed on to the Life Fund. The self-employed will pay their contributions direct to the Life Fund (as they have done to HMRC for National Insurance contributions). Others not in employment but with other income should pay direct to the Life Fund, possibly through a bank standing order if they need to make contributions.

In all cases the sum is deducted from the income otherwise liable to tax. It will therefore be an additional personal allowance. If the official personal allowance is £12,500 it will in practice be raised to £14,500 for those making contributions to the Life Fund. When the individual contributes £40 the state will contribute the same sum to the Life Fund for the same period (say, 40 years) for 50 weeks of the year (£2,000 pa).

The state will in practice pay £1,000 into a member's Life Fund account when that member has made contributions totalling that sum and another £1,000 after the member has made more contributions totalling that sum. At the end of a year £4,000 on this basis will have been credited to the individual's account, £2,000 contributed by the individual and £2,000 contributed by the state.

The Life Fund for 10 years between the ages of 18 and 70 and for every year after the individual reaches the age of 70 years will pay out a fixed sum (say, £160 pw) to the contributor. These payments out to the individual will all be subject to tax. These sums could be paid to the individual in the way agreed by both parties.

The precise number of years in which contributions have to be made, the amount of these contributions and the precise number of years in which payments out can be made and the amount of these payments can be amended after actuarial study. However, the principle of the scheme will not be affected by the result of such investigation.

For the purpose of this study, it will be assumed, as stated above, that the weekly payment by the individual at the start of the scheme will be £40 over 40 years for 50 weeks of the year, whilst the state also contributes £40 per week. The weekly payment out will be £160 over 10 years before the age of 70 and every year beyond the age of 70. These figures will be amended at the end of each financial year to take account of inflation. If there is 3% inflation in the first year, then the weekly contribution in the second year will be £41.20 and weekly payments out will be £164.80.

National Insurance contributions at the moment are regarded, understandably, as tax because they are paid into the state and are not seen to relate precisely to benefits. The Life Fund system is different: every contribution made goes to the credit of one's own account and the sums paid out are directly related to the amount paid in. The state is involved only to the extent to which it pays into the Life Fund (£2,000 pa for 40 years).

At the moment employers contribute to National Insurance on behalf of their employees while self-employed persons make a higher contribution. Under this new scheme, each individual makes the same basic contribution, whether self-employed or employed, while the state pays the same sum to the contributor's fund whether employed or self-employed. Employers no longer have to pay National Insurance but should give £10 per week to their employees to help them make their weekly payment of £40.

(b) Institutions

For reasons set out earlier a system in which autonomous enterprises compete with each other on a level playing field is usually the most efficient way of delivering goods and services, so long as this is consistent with justice and subject to inspection.

There is no reason to suppose that this should not be the case when it comes to the provision of Life Funds. With government help three or four autonomous life fund institutions should first be established as Trusts. These associations will compete for business in operating Life Fund accounts for individuals. Individuals will choose the Life Fund institution they prefer and will be issued with a number. This number will take the place of the existing National Insurance number. Existing financial institutions, such as building societies, would be able to establish Life Fund Management Associations as autonomous trusts to compete with these enterprises. Each individual must have a fund account but can choose the institution to provide it. The Life Fund managers will invest funds received in the best interests of their individual clients; they will also be able to work out and offer terms which involve individual contributions of more than £2,000 pa and payments out of more that £160 per week. The Life Fund Managers will be absolutely committed to the minimum payout of £160 pw (adjusted for inflation) and the state (in return for appointing the Auditors and insisting that their advice is followed where the viability of the business is of concern) will guarantee this. In addition, no interest, dividend, rental or other income received by the Life Fund institutions will be liable to tax or levy (although all payments made to members may count as taxable income). All Life Fund associations will of course be inspected annually so that financial arrangements can be checked.

(c) Flexibility

The Life Fund scheme needs to be flexible (in a way that National Insurance contributions and benefits are not).

It will be possible for someone on low pay to make partial payment for a few months. A man with regular work but on low income may be able to agree to pay £30 pw, (£1500 pa) for a 15 year period, instead of £40 pw (£2,000 pa) for 10 years, giving him 5 additional years in which he has to make a contribution.

Similarly someone in a difficult period will be able to take partial payments out of the fund of the standard £160 pw. A partly employed person could take out £32 pw (£1,600 pa) i.e. 2/10ths of the due payment for 5 years and still only use up one of the 10 years' entitlement before the age of 70.

People receiving an income above their real needs might increase their weekly contribution to £50 pw, say, and so reduce the number of years in which they would have to make a payment. Equally a person on winning the lottery for instance could pay up a much larger sum, (say £20,000) sufficient to cover 10 years in advance.

Someone at the age of 65 may have taken income for 7 years. Such an individual still having 3 payout years unused can agree with the Life Fund Managers not to take out £160 pw for these 3 years, but to take out more than the normal £160pw for each year after 70.

Someone may take out £160 in March to meet a pressing problem and return the same sum in November say. For such irregular payments out it will be reasonable for the Life Fund to make a small charge according to the month in which the payment out occurs and the time taken to repay it.

Again an individual who so wishes could transfer a Life Fund account to a different institution according to pre-ordained rules governing such transfers.

Of course flexibility has its limits. If someone aged 20 wishes to start taking out £160 pw with no family responsibility, with no interest of getting a job or starting at college, then the Life Fund Managers must, in the last resort, have to say no. In any case young people under 30 should not be able to take out more that 6 years' worth of payments except in very special cases which the Life Fund Managers would have to approve.

All individuals would be able at any age to contribute as much as they wish to the Life Fund up to the total sum expected to be paid over 40 years at £2,000 pa, making £80,000. Up to this point the state will contribute the same amount at the same time so that the individual will have a credit of £160,000 after all contributions have been made.

(d) Identification of members

Citizens joining a Life Fund should be given a membership card together with a member identification number (to replace the National Insurance number). Before the number there would be a letter to identify the Life Fund association in which the member is enrolled – the letter to be used would be determined centrally by a body representing all Life Fund associations.

(e) Client Relationships

One of the more unpleasant features of the present means-tested benefit system is the sense of a state bureaucracy issuing long forms to be completed and warding off claimants who are expected to cheat.

Under the scheme proposed, the clients have greater dignity: they can choose which Life Fund Association they want and can change to another Fund if they wish. They have a fixed life-time entitlement so cheating does not arise; whatever happens they can take out only what they are entitled to take. Life Fund Managers will also be expected to appoint Personal Advisers to deal with given individuals, to be able to advise a client not only on Fund payments but also on financial matters generally.

Although a network of Job shops as now will provide details of job opportunities and give advice, the Life Fund association may also advise on training and education courses available. Each person will know that there is someone at the Life Fund office who is able to provide help and advice. Each individual will be able to book an appointment to see or to speak on the 'phone to an advisor. The Life Fund Managers may reasonably make a small charge (deductible from the member's account) for advice given or it could be a part of the service. The charge would not be more than half of a week's pay-out (£80). The Life Fund scheme is flexible but it is also certain: everyone would know how much their assets are worth or could find out after contacting the office.

At the moment many people take out Pay Day loans to enable them to pay their debts on pay day – then take out another loan to pay debts until the following pay day. The Pay Day firms charge high interest on such loans. With the Life Fund people will be able to withdraw their weekly payment of £160 for a few weeks until the debts have been paid – at little or no cost to themselves if they have been making payments into the fund. Millions of British people buy goods and services on credit and face great amounts of debt which inhibit their freedom. They should be able to get impartial advice from the office of their Life Fund Association. Many individuals have problems in paying the rent. They will be able to ask their Life Fund Association for advice

2. How people will be able to pay

The government must ensure that everyone at work earns sufficient to pay £40 pw. The answer is to have a high enough minimum wage.

The minimum or living wage

If people are to feel it worthwhile to work, the pay should be enough to meet their needs. The minimum wage needs to be raised significantly. In his summer budget of the 8th July 2015 the Chancellor of the Exchequer went a long way to meet this need by announcing that the minimum wage for those over 25 would be replaced by a living wage which would be £7.20 in April 2016 and rise to £9 by 2020.

All workers will have to pay their weekly contribution to the Life Fund in place of National Insurance. Those being paid £9 ph will of course be expected to pay in £40 pw and with a minimum weekly wage of £315 for 35 hours, they should be able to do this.

Those under 25, if paid at a lower rate, could perhaps agree to pay the Life Fund less. They could for instance agree to pay £32 pw (£1,600 pa) for 5 years, £8000 in all, instead of £40 pw (£2,000 pa) for 4 years and then have to pay £40 pw for an extra year. However a higher minimum wage must be set for those over 20 and not yet 25, at least £7.50 by 2020.

3. Effect on employment

Under the present system, unemployed people are entitled to benefit but if they take part-time work they are supposed to declare it and lose part or all of the unemployment pay (Jobseeker's Allowance). Hence they may try and do odd work for cash without declaring it.

'The money is there and surely it makes sense to take it?' they may be tempted to think. The system undermines the personal integrity of such people and leads to unnecessary public expenditure.

Under the scheme now proposed there is a clear life-time maximum amount of time during which payment can be taken from the Life Fund. It is in anyone's interest to take as little as needed now in order to keep more in the pot for later. An unemployed man may, perfectly honourably and legally, do odd jobs for part of the week and be paid for it and still take a £160pw payout – or his income may be sufficient to allow him to draw only a part, say 5/10ths of the £160 payout each week. Whatever money is not taken out will be available in the future.

The Life Fund Managers will have the power, subject to appeal, to withhold payments where there is a clear case that such withdrawals will harm the individual in the long term. Moreover the rules should specify that, except in special cases, no one should take out more that 6 years of entitlement before the age of 30.

For 6 months after becoming unemployed people of working age will be entitled to draw out payments from the Life Fund but within 6 months they should either find other employment or begin a training or education course.

It is the state's job to ensure that both employment and such training courses, leading to qualifications, are available.

The state must ensure that jobs are available and if necessary subsidise employment in existing enterprises or, even if more heavily subsidised, employment with such bodies as an environmental task force run by councils. If the state can provide neither training nor employment then it will have to pay direct to the individual 80%, say, of the weekly payment i.e. £128 leaving the individual to take out from the Life Fund a further £32 if available and needed. But this is a situation from which the unemployed person and the tax payer both suffer. It's a failure which good government must avoid.

The facilities offered by the Job Centre Plus are vital to the unemployed person looking for work and are currently run by the state. It should be the state's job to ensure that necessary services are provided but not, if possible, to provide them itself. Responsibility moreover must be undertaken at the lowest level consistent with reasonable efficiency.

Regional or County Councils should take on responsibility for ensuring that the service is effectively provided but invite tenders for autonomous enterprises to be paid for taking on the work. Such enterprises might be given credits (a) for improvement in overall employment levels and (b) for those individuals who have moved from unemployment into a new job at which they have remained for at least three months.

Many existing Job Centres provide a very good service but many other Labour exchanges as they were formally called have been closed down in smaller towns. Consequently many job seekers who live in such areas or in the country have to make long journeys to get the Job Centre. Autonomous enterprises would have the freedom to open offices in smaller towns perhaps just for one or two half days per week.

There should be no unemployment pay or Job Seeker's Allowance. The state will be responsible for ensuring that work or suitable training or education is available.

4. Significance for education

(a) Helping people acquire basic skills

It is possible that some young people may not be accepted for certain jobs because of their low level of general education, in particularly in literacy and numeracy. According to the OEDC report, published in October 2013, young English people came 22nd of 24 developed nations in literacy and 21st in numeracy. This is entirely and predictably the result of mistaken government policy on examinations and the curriculum since the 1990's.

What the government should do is to arrange for a national body to set out the objectives of education for all children with a strong emphasis on literacy and numeracy and then arrange for all children to be assessed first at the age of 15 or so then at 17. Children could also be able to specialise in some subjects but not at the expense of general education. But the government has failed to recognise this.

Instead schools have been told that what matters is how many of their pupils get good grades (A to C) in five specialist GCSE courses. They have responded and an increasing number of students do get good grades.

Heads and teachers know that their reputation and the respect of parents depend on the percentage of their pupils getting good grades in five specialist courses and their position in league tables depends on this. They have to concentrate on the children who may or may not get a good grade and they can afford to neglect the brighter students who will pass anyway and the weakest ones who have no chance of doing so.

As a result, an increasing number of students do get good grades. But schools have been forced to aim for this rather than the good general education of all pupils.

It may be argued that these specialist subjects include Maths and English but numeracy and literacy are only part of the course and you don't need a high percentage to get a good grade.

The answer is of course to have an examination system which will help children to acquire the skills and knowledge which they will all need. Once this is done, young people who have not had the benefit of such a system should be encouraged to take a year's course in general education and to use their Life Fund to pay for their living expenses while they do this.

(b) Living costs for students in higher education

College students used to have a grant from the state to meet living costs, the amount depending on their parent's income. Now students are expected to pay, securing the necessary funds by means of a loan, a loan which must be gradually repaid as the graduate receives sufficient income to do this. Tuition costs is a different matter but it is now generally accepted as reasonable that the state should not pay for the living costs of students. First, most students will become higher than average earners and so should afford to pay. Secondly, it does not seem right that those who do not go to college and subsequently get lower than average incomes receive nothing but contribute through taxes to support the lives of their more fortunate peers. Finally, the loan system relieves the state of what would otherwise be a large financial burden.

On the other hand many reasonable parents bring up their children to avoid debt (except when paying for the appreciating value of a house) and many young people worry about building up a debt. It seems a very bad way to begin adult life.

The Life Fund system avoids this problem. While students are at college their Life Fund Association will be obliged to advance whatever proportion of the weekly out payment is needed, such payments probably to be made every four weeks. Parents who can afford to do so may of course contribute as well and so reduce the amount a student needs to take out from the Life Fund.

Those students who take out their full weekly entitlement for three years will still have seven years in hand to take out money before their 70th birthday. There is a problem for some students, such as those studying medicine and veterinary science, who may have to spend five years at university. But the problem is no greater than it is with the present student loan system. If they have to draw out the maximum £160 pw for 50 weeks each year (£8,000 pa) over five years, this will, it is agreed, constitute a large sum (£40,000). They will still, however, have five of their ten pay out years before 70 available so, if they avoid any further claims, could retire at 65. Qualified doctors or veterinary surgeons moreover are paid at a good salary and could well afford to "buy back" the years during which they have drawn out payments as students.

The Life Fund could also be used for meeting the living costs of those on educational and training courses in later years.

5. Financial viability of the scheme

(a) For the individual and the Life Fund

Using the figures set out above, the individuals must for 40 years pay £40 pw (£2,000 pa) into their Life Fund account. The state pays the same sum at the same time (2,000 pa). After 40 years, the sum paid in will be £160,000, £80,000 from the individual and £80,000 from the state.

Assuming that the average expectation of life is 80 years, the Life Fund will have to make payments of £160 pw or £8,000 pa for 10 years before the age of 70 and 10 years on average after that, 20 years in all, costing it £160,000 for the average individual. So the total outlay equals the total income for the Life Fund.

For the Life Fund institutions this should be financially viable. They will of course invest the money and the income from capital growth from these investments should yield sufficient to pay out for the 51st and 52nd weeks at Christmas as well as the £160 per week for an average of 20 years.

The Life Fund association moreover will not be taxed on the returns it gets from its investments. Tax will be paid by individual members when they receive their payments.

It must also be recognised that most people pay early in life and take out later when the payment will have been inflation indexed. Even so, so long as the auditors are happy, a Life Fund could commit itself to making the payments required.

Since this income is vital for the individual when he needs it there must be 100% security. The state will have to accept that if the Life Fund should ever be in a position where it cannot pay out then it would make an interest free loan to the Fund to tide it over in its difficulties; in return the FCA (Financial Conduct Authority) must have the right to examine the auditor's annual accounts and to offer advice which in the last resort might be binding.

If the work of the Life Fund Association, the advice and support it gives its members, demands more staff then to meet the costs it would be possible to ask members to make their payment of £40 pw not only for 50 weeks but also for a 51st week, direct to the Life Fund Association to pay for its services. The Life Fund Association may also be able to call on qualified volunteers to give advice to its members.

(b) For the state and the taxpayer

The state will have to contribute £40 pw (£2,000 pa) for all individuals over the 40 years during which they contributes to the Life Fund, i.e. £80,000 in all. Assuming that the average expectation of life is 80, then the state contributes for half each person's lifetime on average. If there is a population of 64 million then at any point half (32 million) would be entitled to this receipt, total payments for the year £2,000 x 32m = £64 bn.

The state will have to contribute certain additional sums to support families with children and to support insurance payments to protect people from disability. But the total of such additional payments would certainly not be more than £35 bn. The total expenditure would be well under £100 bn, well below the present cost. According to figures published by the Treasury and reported in the Times (9/7/15) the total cost of benefits for 2015/16 was in fact more than £216 bn. The Department of Work and Pensions is in fact the biggest spending department in the UK.

The state will have no need to pay any of the benefits, pensions, Jobseeker's Allowance, Income Support, Council Tax Benefit, Tax Credits and Housing benefits. The cost to the state will be far less than it pays out to support the current system of social security.

The change in the position of the taxpayer is even more remarkable. Under the present social security system the taxpayer meets the cost of around £215 bn pa. Under the Life Fund system each citizen, whether a tax payer or not, pays in £40 pw for 40 years and the state pays £40 pw for 40 years into each citizen's Life Fund account. All citizens receive as much as they pay in.

So there will be a system without means-testing in which everyone can expect to receive a payment of £160 pw (index linked) after the age of 70 and for 10 years before that to cover, in particular, periods of education after 18 and unemployment – at a cost to the state much less than what it pays out at the moment.

NB: The Life Fund will not need to make payments to its members (except in the short term) to those who are prevented from working by injury or illness and who currently receive the Employment Support Allowance or

Disability Living Allowance (Personal Independence Payment). This will be covered by insurance (below).

6. *Altering the terms of the contract*

All payments will be adjusted for inflation so there should not be need for adjustment. However the operation of the scheme will have to be reviewed every few years and changes can be made so long as they do not harmfully affect those who have already enrolled.

7. *Introduction of the Life Fund*

(a) Registration of 18 year olds

Initially, in the first year of its operation, all citizens aged 18 will be expected to register with the Life Fund institution of their choice. If they are beginning a course of higher or further education they will be able to draw out weekly payments from their Life Fund account. If they are starting work they will normally be expected to pay in their £40 pw which will be matched by £40 from the state – although the payment could be higher or lower if they so wish.

Parents may choose to make payments in on behalf of their children taking advantage of the fact that such payments are removed from their taxable income and added to their personal allowance. These payments could be made in advance while their child is still 16 or 17 years old.

(b) Registration after 18

Strictly speaking, the operation of the Life Fund is designed to deal with individuals throughout their working life and beyond. Those aged 18 join while those over that age simply carry on with the present system. However the Life Fund system is so much better that we must try to enable older people to join too.

For those younger adults who have not yet paid national insurance it is a question of making the same deal as that involving 18 year olds. They must pay £40 pw for 40 years and will be eligible to receive £160 pw for 10 years before 70 and every year after that. A young man aged 25 can start paying £40 pw and carry on doing so until he's 65. He will be able to draw out £160 pw like every other younger member for 10 years before the age of 70 and for every year after that.

For those who have paid national insurance it would seem fair to credit them with payment made into the Fund. Someone who has paid national insurance of £10 pw (£500 pa) for four years would receive a credit of £2,000 which would be given to the Life Fund to cover one year's payment.

A man aged 40 who has paid national insurance for 20 years at around £10 pw (£500 pa) would receive a credit of £10,000 which would be transferred to the Life Fund to cover 5 years at £2,000 pa and the state would pay in the same amount to this account.

The 40 year old man would still have to make payments of £40 pw for another 35 years. But he would be entitled to receive payments of £160 pw for 10 years before reaching the age of 70. He simply has to make a plan with his Life Fund to reconcile his obligation with his entitlement. He could for instance agree to use 5 years of his entitlement (£160 pw) to pay for 20 years of his obligation to pay £40 pw. In each of these 5 years he would draw out £160 pw (£8,000 pa) and use this to make 4 years of payments of £40 pw (£8,000 pa). The state has to match this payment of £40 pw. It still seems a good deal. The man still has to pay in £40 pw for another 20 years but he still has 5 more years in which to take out £160 pw as well as for every year after he is 70.

A woman aged 50 who has paid national insurance for 24 years at around £10 pw (£500 pa) would receive a credit of £12,000 which would be transferred to her Life Fund to cover 6 years at £2,000 and the state must pay in the same amount. Over the next 20 years she will be obliged to make 40 payments of £40 pw and be entitled to receive 10 years of £160 pw. She could choose to take out payments of £160 pw for seven years giving her £8,000 for each of these years (£56,000 in all) and use this sum to make payments of £40 pw (£2,000 pa) over 28 years (28 x £2,000 = £56,000). After these 7 years, at the age of 57, she will still have to make payments of £40 pw for 12 years and be able to take out £160 pw for 3 years.

So it is possible for her to enrol with a Life Fund Association.

However people aged over 55 should have the option of whether or not they should try and join a Life Fund and Life Funds should be able to decide whether or not to accept them. If they can not be accepted, they must continue to pay national insurance and they will receive their pension from the state. If there are those over 30 but below 55 years old who are not happy with the Life Fund, they might be allowed to make arrangements with an autonomous trust with whom they would save for a pension and insure themselves against needs arising if unemployed or otherwise prevented from working. They should pay at least £40 pw (£2,000 pa) into such a policy for up to 40 years in which case the state would make similar payments for the same number of years.

8. The need for national acceptance of the Life Fund system

Clearly a major change in the social security system would require general support so that individuals do not have anything to fear from the results of the next General Election. Anyone who opposes it should be asked to read

Part 1 of this book. How can British people possibly support a system so full of injustice, vulnerability to fraud and general muddle?

Opponents of the Life Fund system should try and devise an alternative, not defend the present system.

9. *Relevance of the European Union*

It may be argued that the radical changes proposed in this book may not be entirely consistent with the rules of the European Union.

If the difference is minimal, this may be resolved. If however the difference is significant then this should lead to Britain's withdrawal from the political aspect of the European Union. British people must not be denied the right to decide for themselves the way they are to be governed.

On the other hand the Life Fund system may make continued membership of the European Union more acceptable to Britain. The EU rules say that citizens from other EU states must be entitled to the same rights and benefits as those in their country of residence. If British citizens are entitled to benefits such as the Jobseeker's Allowance then eastern Europeans in Britain must also qualify for this benefit. But to many Britons it does not seem right that immigrants should be able to receive such benefits.

The Life Fund system removes this problem. Other EU nationals will be in the same position as British people.

Immigrants who are young enough and who wish to stay in Britain may open a Life Fund account. Those who are on short visits should be required to insure themselves with a European or British insurance firm. It is necessary that a new insurance institution should be established and immigrants would be expected to register.

They must pay the sum required and will get financial help if the need arises. There will be no payments from social security. Immigrants wishing to settle in Britain who have paid insurance contributions in their former country will be in the same position as those in Britain who have paid national insurance. The government which has received the contributions must transfer part or all of them to the Life Fund to help pay the weekly sums due. Older immigrants moving to Britain may not be able to join a Life Fund. They should also insure with a British insurance firm, paying so much a month or week and receiving financial support in time of need.

C   Compulsory insurance for long-term incapacity or disability

For expected and not entirely unexpected needs, the Life Fund provides the answer: up to a specific sum (say £160 pw) in short-term unemployment, when engaged in full-time and perhaps part-time education, during short periods of illness and in old age.

But situations may arise in which this is not enough and access to a larger sum and/or over a much longer period is required. Illness or injury may involve prolonged even life long disability and in this situation, if the individual is to retain independence, additional income is required.

At the moment the state provides support for such long term illness and disability, through the Employment Support Allowance or Personal Independence Plan.

There is however, a widespread view that doctors certify too readily that a person is unable to work and should therefore receive benefits. It is also alleged that governments have been happy to go along with this since such a person no longer appears in the unemployment statistics.

But benefit, as explained above, has been increasingly paid to people with mental or behavioural problems who may need special help in returning to work.

The answer is that each individual must insure against the possibility of incapacity and disability.

Insurance Societies must be established, some perhaps by the Life Fund Association and each citizen will be obliged to register and insure with these societies. The citizen will be obliged to pay so much each month to the insurance society. This payment will be made from income that would otherwise be taxed. If the personal allowance is £12,500, then the first £2,000 above that will be used for 40 years to make the citizen's Life Fund payments. If the insurance payment due is £20 pcm (£240 pa) that will be paid from income above £14,500 so tax will only be paid on income above

£14,740. If the citizens do not have income over £14,500 then the state pays it on their behalf. Once the due payment has been made the citizens will receive an insurance voucher.

They will use the voucher to insure with the insurance society of their choice. All such insurance societies must operate as autonomous trusts.

The society is then responsible for making payments to them when unable to work because of physical incapacity. Since the society can only spend from the income it receives it will be very careful to check that the claimant is unable to work. If claimants have mental health problems, the society will ensure that they have opportunity for treatment and are given part time work if this seems desirable.

The society will also see what sort of work the claimant might undertake, some way of earning money in addition to what the society may pay. The society may agree at first that the money so earned can be kept in addition to the payment it provides. Gradually however the money earned by the claimant should make payment from the society unnecessary.

If the claimants are unable to work because of obesity, then the society should only provide support if they are taking measures to reduce it. The society will be expected to treat those who are addicted to alcohol or drugs in the same way.

Legal Expenses Insurance

Legal Aid is a means-tested benefit and therefore unfair. It is also a questionable use of taxpayer's money. The answer is compulsory insurance for legal expenses. The cost could be under £30 pa and could be paid through the Life Fund. Autonomous Trusts would be established, perhaps by the Life Fund Association, which would receive the insurance payment and cover legal costs should the need arise up to a fixed maximum of say £200,000. If a client needs legal representation for more than 2 or 3 times then the Insurance society would raise the charge. In extreme cases, the client would be referred to the State.

D. Family Support

1. The care of young children

The most important task that any society has is to bring up the children well so that they will in due course become good citizens contributing to society in the future. The state as the agent of society must take measures and spend money to facilitate this process.

At the moment the state provides various benefits to help parents as part of the social security system. These include Child Benefit, Maternity Allowance, tax credits, childcare allowance and support for lone parents This is the wrong way to operate financial support for parents. Family Support should be the responsibility of a new mini-department with its own minister in charge. The existing benefits must be removed and be replaced by a new system of family support which concentrates on measures to give children the best possible start in life.

Both logic and the evidence support the view that, all other things being equal, the child does best if brought up in a family home by the natural parents. The state must put children first and should therefore create such conditions as most favour the child's development. The key is to ensure that young children have a close contact with parents.

Important evidence for this has been provided by the Nobel Prize winning economist and child development expert, James Hackman, author of 'The American family in black and white', published in 2012. He has drawn on the work of neuro-scientists who have found that the brain is only partly developed at birth and that what happens in the first few years determines how well it develops. An essential element in this development is the close attachment of the child to a loving parent, normally the mother, in a long-term personal relationship. What happens in the first 5 years of life is far more important than later years in determining the sort of person the child will become and this depends on close attachment. If the mother or father is not closely involved with the child in these years the brain will not develop its full potential.

What must be done therefore is to ensure that for children under 5 there must always be a parent available – as was expected in the middle of the twentieth century.

The presence or absence of a parent being home after school is also a vital factor affecting the way children and teenagers develop. The state must create conditions in which the children grow up where possible with loving parents available throughout their childhood years

2. *Binding partnership contracts*

The state must invite all men and women planning to have children to agree to and sign a binding contract of partnership in which both parties promise (a) to provide jointly a common family home at least until their youngest child reaches the age of 18 and (b) to be faithful to each other. As part of the contract, both parents will be required to attend a parenting course before the birth of their first child and at least one of them required to attend further every few years. Where such contracts exist the state will require that the parents open a joint bank account, although in some cases this may be a basic account, without a cheque book. The state will then pay £100 per week into this account so long as a child under 5 lives in the house and the contract holds and so long as one parent is always available for the child during the week. It should pay £50 pw so long as a child under 16 lives in the house and one parent is available at home after 2pm. Both parents of a child under 5 may wish to continue with their work. In that case they must ask for their terms of employment to be around 20 hours a week and employers must be legally bound to meet this request. This would enable at least one parent to be available for the child every day. Parents will of course also receive an additional sum of £40 for the first child, £30 for a second and third child but not more than £10 for any subsequent child. One or both parents would also put money into this account and take money out of the Life Fund if needed.

A contractual partnership will also define the financial circumstances of the partnership. First, all capital assets belonging to either partner will continue to belong to that partner as will legacies received thereafter. Secondly, all income earned by either partner from the date of the contract will belong equally to both parties and will be banked or invested in their joint names. Thirdly, the partnership will be taxed as such, with both parties providing details of their income in the same document. If the personal tax allowance is £12,500 then so long as there is one child under 16 in the household the tax allowance for the partnership will be £18,000, say, whether both partners work or just one does. This situation will mean that the family where one partner stays at home to look after children will not be disadvantaged as is the case at the moment.

If the father is the only income earner he and the family will enjoy a personal allowance of £18,000 rather than £12,500 as for a single person.

3. Uncontracted parents

Even if no contract is signed, both parents must be jointly responsible for a child born as a result of their sexual relations. It is an accepted maxim that people must take responsibility for the consequences of their action. Should there be any doubts, the father can if necessary be identified by DNA testing and he will be required each week to make a payment from his Life Fund account or bank account to be paid into the mother's account. The non-resident parent will be required to pay an increasing sum to the mother's or other carer's account until the child is 16.

A new child support agency must ensure that the appropriate sum is paid out of the non-resident parent's bank or Life Fund account into that of the parent actually caring for the child. The caring parent will also receive £40 pw for the first child, £30 pw for the second and third child and £10 pw for any subsequent child.

The mother may also need to ask for money to be transferred from her Life Fund account into her bank account.

E. Housing

The section on housing in the first part of this book has shown how much waste and injustice is involved in housing benefit. It must be put in the rubbish bin with all the other benefits. Other ways must be found to ensure that everyone has a decent home. The provision must be based on principles.

1. *Principles*

Each individual member of society needs a home to provide shelter and warmth, furnishings and equipment; it is a vital part of the physical circumstances necessary to the life of an individual whether living alone or in a family or other group.

The good society is one of free and independent citizens who are able to secure such facilities for themselves and their families.

Citizens should be free to live where they wish insofar as accommodation is available and so long as they have sufficient means. They should be able to choose whether to rent their home or, if they can afford to do so, to own it.

People are best served if different enterprises are able to compete as autonomous trusts to provide the best possible service or product at the most reasonable price. Different enterprises should compete to provide homes for rent and for sale. All such enterprises must be able in the medium term to secure sufficient income to cover their costs.

The role of government, whether central or local, should not be to provide homes but to ensure that the conditions exist for citizens to be able to choose accommodation for themselves, whether by purchase or rent, in particular to manage the housing market to ensure that as far as possible people of limited means are able to secure such housing. The government must also ensure that sufficient housing is available. What must be done is to show how housing can be provided in a way consistent with these principles.

2. Houses for rent

Council houses

During the twentieth century the construction of council houses became the main route to the provision of cheap subsidised housing for renting to those on low incomes and insofar as this is concerned they have performed a useful function. In the early 1970's there were 5 million such homes.

However, the public is best served if enterprises compete to provide the best service or product and individuals can select which suits them best. Monopoly provision whether by central government or by a private body should be avoided for the reasons set out earlier.

It would be unsatisfactory even if the council were one provider competing with independent bodies, since the council does not have to make ends meet in its provision of housing in the way independent bodies have to do.

As councils provide accommodation at less that the commercial rate, many people will want to secure one. This places the councillors and officers who run the system in a position of power while potential tenants are supplicants who may feel that a gift or recollection of a past friendship will help their cause. Councils often use a system which places applicants in a rough sort of order on the basis of points scored (e.g. for children). Even so it is the provider choosing the purchaser when it should be the other way 'round. Because it is a financially good deal, council tenants once established do not want to move if they can help it unless they can find an equally good deal elsewhere: this then reduces the flexibility of labour which is so helpful to the economy.

Kate David, Chief Executive of Notting Hill Housing, writing in The Times (14/11/08), questioned the practice of letting council houses for the lifetime of the tenant. "A tenancy for life might be right for someone who is elderly or disabled, where the chance of them getting a job and being able to look after themselves could be nil, but to write someone off as a teenager, I think, is really sad. A third of all social lettings are to people under the age of 25. In London, for every home available there can be 200 people applying."

The basic position of a monopoly provider, the local council, letting homes to people at less that the market rate is grossly unfair.

Peter Marsh, appointed first head of the Tenant Services Authority (TSA) on 1st December 2008, was also critical of the current arrangements for rented housing (The Times 28/11/08). He argued that many of the people in social rented housing shouldn't be there in the first place, that many were too rich and should have been offered alternatives, such as shared equity or private rented accommodation. He questioned why social tenants in Central London paid £70 to £100 a week to rent a flat, while private tenants would pay £800 a week for a similar property or £1,000 a week for a fixed-term mortgage.

The truth is that the participation of councils in the provision of rented housing creates unacceptable injustices. There must be a free market in rented housing but managed to ensure that the poor do not lose out.

For councils to provide housing for rent is to create an unfair market with other suppliers at a disadvantage. Council ownership of housing for rent must then be replaced by alternative forms of provision. Indeed this process has been in train for some time: the number of council houses has fallen significantly thanks partly to the sale of houses to tenants and partly to the transfers already made to housing associations and trusts.

Transfer of council houses to other operators

In accordance with the principle that people are best served if two or more autonomous enterprises independent of the state offer competing services, each council must be required to dispose of any remaining housing by dividing its estate into three or more geographical blocks and offering them for sale for refurbishment or replacement with the provisos that (a) the rent will not initially be more than a fixed sum, agreed by the council, (b) that the rent for existing tenants will not for a specified period of, say, three years rise by more than the cost of living index in any given year unless there has been a major refurbishment and (c) that existing adult tenants over the age of 40 all have security of tenure for their lifetime so long as they pay rent and are not found guilty by a court of anti-social behaviour. The council will then accept the best offer considering not only the amount of the bid but the competence of the bidder.

Housing Associations

Housing associations were established by the Thatcher government to take over council housing estates where the majority of tenants voted for this.

There were more than 1,500 of them in 2015. As Channel 4 demonstrated on the 23rd July 2015, this administrative system is unnecessarily expensive while the top people are excessively well paid.

Before they bid for the council houses, they should be converted into autonomous trusts. Their main purpose must be the welfare of their tenants so long as fair rents are properly paid. Their income must in the medium term be sufficient to cover their costs.

They will need money to buy council houses. For this they must turn to the Housing Corporation.

Housing Corporation

The Housing Corporation was established to provide money to the housing association. Some other Housing Corporations should now be established to compete with the first, operating on the same terms. All must operate as autonomous trusts.

Like the housing associations which they support they must in the medium term derive sufficient income to meet their costs. They must provide loans to housing associations to enable them to acquire houses to let.

Securing Finance

First the Housing Corporation must borrow money from the state. For the state therefore this must be a loan, an investment, not a grant. Given existing problems the interest rate must be low, say 1.7 per cent.

Let us say that a housing association is acquiring 10 houses each costing £150,000. The Housing Corporation could lend this sum at 1.8 per cent so that the housing associations will have to pay £2,700 pa interest on the loan for each house. Rental payments for such homes should be sufficient to cover the borrowing costs of the housing association and to help it build up capital. A rent of £60 per week would cover the borrowing costs, so tenants might be asked to pay £70 pw. When the house is occupied by a family such payments should be possible if there are two contracted partners, one of them working, with family support.

If their income is insufficient, one or both of the contracted partners should be able to draw out some money from their Life Fund accounts. Instead of drawing out £160 pw for one year, they could draw out £32 pw say over five years or even £16 pw over 10 years and still use only one year's entitlement.

Housing associations must of course also ensure that there are sufficient single rooms to let to one person as tenant.

The Housing Corporations must have the capacity to build houses themselves. Building firms like to build houses that appeal to the wealthy but the Housing Corporation must build low-cost houses that are so needed. The Housing Corporation would then sell these to a housing association which will rent them out.

Capital Repayment

The housing association will be expected to repay the capital to the Housing Corporation and the Housing Corporation to the state within 50 years

So what happens to those on housing benefit?

After the Life Fund system has been introduced, those on housing benefit should be told that payments must cease after 6 months. During this period representatives of the local council should see all those affected and advise them on what they should do. They will help them contact the housing association which will now be responsible for the house in which they live.

There are many young people under 25 who receive housing benefit while they seek to acquire useful skills and prepare for a career. They can take out up to £160 pw from their Life Fund account which with some work remuneration should cover the cost of board and lodging in the one room required.

Many of the people receiving housing allowances live in London. Either the employer must pay more or they must move out to somewhere where housing is cheaper. Many professional people expect to move around between appointments and the children have to go to different schools. It's not a terrible burden.

3. Houses for purchase

Lower cost of houses is of course important, not just for those who want to rent them but also for those who want to own their home and have to borrow the money usually with a mortgage which means a heavy monthly payment to the bank or building society.

To raise the money both parents often work instead of undertaking the far more important task of bringing up their children with one of them being at home for them at least until they reach the age of 5. Action must be taken therefore to enable more people to be able to own their home, without the need for both parents to work.

The Housing Corporation could, on behalf of the state, buy a stake in the houses on sale. If the house is purchased for £200,000 the Housing Corporation could on behalf of the state bear half the cost (£100,000) and would hold a half-share in the value of the house. If the house is to be sold the Housing Corporation must agree the terms and be entitled to half the amount paid. The Housing Corporation could charge 2%, say, annually on the sum it has provided. From the state's point of view, this could be a good investment if housing prices continue to rise.

Those who live in the house and the bank or other lender will jointly own one half of the house until the occupants have paid all their debt to the lender and become full owners of their half of the house. They will then have the opportunity if they so wish to buy the other half from the Housing Corporation.

Easier finance for home buyers will also help those who have to rent since some home owners will make their housing available for rent. A long term loan of up to £100,000 could be provided by Housing Corporations for those who own flats or houses which they rent out. The interest charged would be the same, say 2%. If the house is sold then the amount borrowed on this low cost loan is repayable to the Housing Corporation which may, however, offer it to the new owners if required.

4. Council/Property Tax

The problems arising from the council tax have been explained in the section on Council Tax Benefit/Support. Local authorities decide for themselves how much discount on council tax there should be for low income families. People living in one town may get a reasonable discount while others in very similar circumstances in another town may get no discount. The councils do not reveal how they work it out. This is totally unacceptable.

The key is the fact that the people who have to pay council tax are the tenants not the owners.

What must be done is to make house owners pay a property tax (to take the place of Council Tax) whether they live in the house or not. Of course this means that the arrangements for determining rent have to be amended. The tenant will no longer pay council or property tax so will have to pay a somewhat higher rent to the landlord who will have to pay the tax

The Property Tax would have to be collected by the councils but then passed to central government at a discount to cover collection costs. But no Council or Property tax benefit or discount will be necessary.

5. Availability of houses

Britain built fewer than half the 240,000 homes that the building industry believes are needed each year to address the shortage. Housing experts have said that the paucity of supply is pushing up prices to unsustainable levels.

The Housing Corporations will be expected to use its own building section to build more lower cost housing but will also take note of the number of homes being built by existing firms so that it can make sure that at least 250,000 houses are built each year so long as the shortage lasts. It should be the responsibility of housing associations to ensure that existing housing is sufficiently used. For instance many old people live alone and have a spare room while young people find it difficult to secure an affordable home.

Adam Sage reported in the Times (10/6/15) on how students were staying with old people in Paris:

A growing number of students are living with elderly people under a scheme launched by charities and being promoted by the French government. Officials see intergenerational housing as a solution for students unable to afford normal digs and for lonely pensioners. The rents tend to be low – as little as €35 for a room in Paris, for example, compared with double that on the free market. Some rooms are free, with the student agreeing in return to spend time chatting with the landlord each day. "This sort of thing has existed for generations but now it is becoming structured", said Makkio Yanno, the director of Le Pari Solidaire, an association which pioneered the concept in France a decade ago. She said her association was inundated with requests from students wanting to live with elderly people in Paris and other cities. "We only accept those who really want to create a relationship and refuse those who apply only because they want a cheap rent." Most of those seeking tenants were widows living alone for the first time, she said. "But we've discovered that many students arriving to live in Paris feel lonely. They want to be with a sort of a family."

In case things go wrong, it would be sensible for the housing association to keep a record of all such arrangements setting out what if anything the lodger should pay and what he or she should contribute to the main occupant of the house. The housing association should also be responsible for checking if houses are left empty for more than 6 months and for persuading the owners to let them out for a specific period on the understanding that if the tenants did not wish to leave at the end of the period the housing association would be responsible for getting them out at the right time and providing alternative accommodation.

Private Letting

Where a landlord or company owns houses for rent on a considerable scale then the operation of the business must become an autonomous trust, with its main purpose being the welfare of the tenant.

A housing association will be established which will borrow money from the housing corporation in order to purchase the house from the former owner, who may now play a leading part in the operation of the new housing association.

In the middle years of the second decade of the twenty first century there has been a considerable increase in the number of individuals buying one or two houses to let, perhaps a few more.

Landlords who just have a small number of houses to rent should be required to register with a housing association. The housing association will ensure that, as with its own housing, there is a proper tenancy agreement giving the details of rent to be paid and of arrangements for the landlord to terminate the contract.

In the summer of 2015 Channel 5 presented a programme 'Nightmare Tenants, Slum Landlords' which showed how both tenants and landlords may abuse their position. If all such tenancies are registered with a housing association then landlords or tenants that feel badly treated will be able to bring their problems to the association which will try and find an answer to the problem.

www.ingramcontent.com/pod-product-compliance
Lightning Source LLC
Chambersburg PA
CBHW072138270326
41931CB00010B/1798

9 7 8 1 8 4 5 4 9 6 7 7 7